Managing Inventory

The One Day Lead Time Process

❖

❖

❖

Managing Inventory

The One Day Lead Time Process

Managing Inventory

The One Day Lead Time Process

David P. Zimmerman

Unlimited Publishing
Bloomington, Indiana

Copyright © 2002 by David P. Zimmerman

Distributing Publisher:
Unlimited Publishing, LLC
Bloomington, Indiana

http://www.unlimitedpublishing.com

Cover and Book Design by Charles King
Copyright © 2001 by Unlimited Publishing, LLC
This book was typeset with Adobe® InDesign®.

All rights reserved under Title 17, U.S. Code, International and Pan-American Copyright Conventions. No part of this work may be reproduced or transmitted in any form or by any means, electronic or mechanical, including photocopying, scanning, recording or duplication by any information storage or retrieval system without prior written permission from the author(s) and publisher(s), except for the inclusion of brief quotations with attribution in a review or report. Requests for permission or further information should be addressed to the author(s).

Unlimited Publishing LLC provides worldwide book design, printing, marketing and distribution services for professional writers and small to mid-size presses, serving as distributing publisher. Sole responsibility for the content of each work rests with the author(s) and/or contributing publisher(s). The opinions expressed herein may not be interpreted in any way as representing those of Unlimited Publishing, nor any of its affiliates.

Copies of this book and others
are available to order online, anytime at:

http://www.unlimitedpublishing.com/authors

ISBN 1-58832-030-8

Unlimited Publishing
Bloomington, Indiana

Dedication

I dedicate this book to all buyers, planners, salespersons, and production supervisors who have fought the good fight to meet their customer's needs. May this book give you one less worry.

Acknowledgements

This work would not be possible without the help and encouragement of many individuals throughout the years. First, I thank my wife, who has always been there for me. Next, Lyudmila Shusterman, who first encouraged me to pursue this topic and smoothed out many paths along the way. Then, Vince Andrews, who allowed me to apply these concepts to real life situations, then to debug and improve them for the production line. Last, but not least, Tom Warda who believes in spite of the naysayers of our world, and never lets me give up. To those who have disagreed with these concepts and practices I also express my thanks, for you have kept me honest and forced me to continuously reexamine my presentations to insure I say what I think I am saying.

Contents

Foreword • ix
Introduction • xi

Chapters

- **1:** Why Lead Times Exist • 1
- **2:** Lead Time Criteria • 7
- **3:** Cycle Time • 19
- **4:** How We Got Here Or, When We Do What We Did, We Get What We Got • 27
- **5:** Cycle Time vs. Lead Time • 39
- **6:** The Effects of Lead Time Lengths • 51
- **7:** Quantifying the Effects of Lead Time Length • 63
- **8:** Capacity and Lead Time • 77
- **9:** Buyer's Effect on Quoted Lead Time • 87
- **10:** Lead Time Drivers • 95
- **11:** The Effects of Inventory on Lead Time • 117
- **12:** Summary • 125
- **13:** Planning Systems and Inventory • 133
- **14:** Use of Planned Excess Raw Material Inventory to Reduce Lead Time (Practical Lead Time Calculation) • 143
- **15:** Safety Stock Calculation • 153
- **16:** Adaptive Master Scheduling (AMS) • 161
- **17:** Item Level Master Scheduling (ILMS) • 183
- **18:** Negotiating with Vendors • 193
- **19:** Electronic Commerce • 203
- **20:** Vendor Managed Inventories (VMI) • 209
- **21:** Wrap-up • 219
- **22:** Managing Inventory with an Integrated Supply Chain • 229

❖

❖

❖

Foreword

Businesses magnify the effects of a recession when they reduce output to reduce inventories in response to lessening demand. That is reacting to the market not managing inventory. A better approach involves businesses cutting output in response to demand without the inventory between them. The problem is the speed of communications between businesses and customers. That speed is measured in the quantity of inventory between the business and the customer, and at the customers' site. Federal Reserve Chairman Alan Greenspan testified before Congress on February 28, 2001 about the then perceived recession, *"Because the extent of the slowdown was not anticipated by businesses, it induced some backup in inventories, despite the more advanced just-in-time technologies that have in recent years enabled firms to adjust production levels more rapidly to changes in demand. ... Reflecting these growing imbalances, manufacturing purchasing managers reported last month that inventories in the hands of their customers had risen to excessively high levels."* He further testified that *"New technologies for supply-chain management and flexible manufacturing imply that businesses can perceive imbalances in inventories at a very early stage—virtually in real time—and can cut production promptly in response to the developing signs of unintended inventory building. Our most recent experience with some inventory backup, of course, suggests that surprises can still occur and that this process is still evolving."* Or, businesses that are unable to respond quickly to demand changes still suffer the effects of recession, and the processes to increase responsiveness are still evolving. This book is a step in the evolution and is based on the following logic path:

- Inventory exists as a buffer between changing customer demands and the inability of a vendor to react to customer demand changes.
- The traditional measure used to track the ability, or the inability, of a vendor to react to customer demand change is lead time.
- The measure of lead time is amount of inventory held by a vendor *and* a customer in order to compensate for lead time length.

Managing inventory then is managing lead time. Said another way, those businesses that systemically reduce the time from customer demand to completed production while minimizing the quantity of inventory between themselves and their customers, and at their customers, do a better job of inventory management.

This book is the result my successful efforts in reducing Lead Time in a production environment from an average of 100 days to 1 day. I accomplished the reduction in three months. The concepts I developed are compensation techniques that resulted in inventory and cost reductions freeing up resources needed for longer term Cycle Time reductions programs, the real key to responsiveness and inventory management.

Introduction

Imagine what your professional life would be like if all Lead Time lengths were One Day.

That slide greeted each new member of my class as they entered the conference room. I heard each mutter about how much easier life would be if only that were true.

It was 8:00 AM and time to start the class and switch slides.

I started, "Better yet, don't imagine, I'm going to show you that."

I started to flip and read slides that said:

- One Day Lead Times generate cost savings:
    - One Day Lead Times reduce procurement costs by one-half to two-thirds.
    - One Day Lead Times reduce production planning costs by one-half to two-thirds.
    - One Day Lead Times reduce sales costs by one-half to two-thirds.
    - One Day Lead Times reduce inventory costs by one-half to two-thirds.
- Any link in a supply chain achieves One Day Lead Times only after it acknowledges that quoted Lead Times lengths are the result of a business decision, not the result of a calculation.
- Adopting the One Day Lead Time process systemically integrates all links in a supply chain.

- Adopting the One Day Lead Time process protects each link in a supply chain from the excess inventories that can result from decreased customer demands. It shortens the communication time between supply and customers minimizing the effects of a recession.

"If those statements do not get your attention, then you are in the wrong place. Move on, save your time and money. But if they do, and you are wondering how, or if, I can back them up; let us begin."

I looked out at my new class and saw the same expressions that I had seen in other classes. Some seemed as if they were there only because their boss told them to attend. Others sat up as they read the overhead and were ready to go. I continued.

"The One Day Lead Time process starts with building a business case (education), because changing paradigms is like changing comfortable shoes, there had better be good reasons to change or the old shoes will be dug out and worn again. The buyer and the vendor must agree on the advantages of changing the way they do business. The next phase in the process is compensation, a method that quickly yields desired results but is incomplete in itself. Finally we will learn how to expand and manage the entire process."

"The education phase starts with an examination of the planning system. Planning systems exist as a tool to aid in the smooth operation of an organization. They predict when actions can start, and calculate expected finish dates and, the effects of delays on finish dates. To accomplish these tasks planning systems use Lead Times, time elements provided by the user of the planning system. Each task has a Lead Time associated with it. That Lead Time may, or may not, be related to the Cycle Time required to perform the task. Understanding and agreeing to these truths is the first step in the education process."

As I look out, I see foreheads furrow and eyebrows lower a sure sign of questions.

"I know that these points raise some questions in your mind. Hold on to them for now. As we progress you will have ample opportunity to ask your questions, to disagree, or to expand on each issue we cover."

I continue.

"Why do I care about Lead Time length? As Lead Time lengths increase costs increase, demands for flexibility (responsiveness) in production planning (manufacturing schedules) from customers increase. Typically, vendors meet these demands for increased responsiveness with increased inventory. Costs increase as inventory levels increase. When the vendor does not use inventory as a tool to increase responsiveness, transactional activities, or clerical activities, needed to control changes to open orders increase as customers attempt to control the quantity of inventory they carry to shield themselves against increased lead times. The statement that inventory levels increase presupposes that one knows what their inventory level should be. To insure that is the case I will, devote a fair amount of time demonstrating how to calculate the inventory levels you currently plan to carry."

"Transactional costs increase because you need to react to changing buyer needs over time. The longer the Lead Time the further into the future the buyer needs to forecast needs. The longer a forecast period, the higher the probability and number, of changes to forecasted needs (dates and quantities). The Lead Times loaded in a planning system limit the ability to react. Customers, therefore, attempt to improve on those Lead Times using any method at their disposal. Transactional costs are the costs incurred as vendors attempt to react to changing customer needs.

You either confirm or reject the requested changes, but in either case, someone must investigate to determine which reaction is appropriate. Again, I will show how to calculate transactional costs based on Lead Time lengths. These costs (inventory and transactional) define the cost of Lead Time. I prove that no one wins with long Lead Times because the increased costs of inventory and transactional activity affect the buyer and the vendor. By the way" I add, "you'll discover that the quantity of inventory you currently maintain is 2, 3 even 4 times what you need or intend to maintain."

"Building on that base", I continue, "I'll examine the time element used by the planning system, Lead Time. What is it, and what is its relationship to Cycle Time? The buyer and vendor look at Lead Time and Cycle Time based on their experience. Buyers and vendors sometimes consider Lead Time and Cycle Time as interchangeable terms but at least they 'know' that Lead Time is driven by Cycle Time. I am going to demonstrate that the conclusions buyers and vendors draw from their experiences are erroneous. That when Cycle Times lengths drive quoted Lead Times lengths the results are added costs and the neutering of their planning systems. At this point, the buyer and vendor will understand their planning system and the time elements used by it."

I see the skepticism in the eyes and body language of the class. Experience has taught them the relationship between Lead Time and Cycle Time, am I going to attack that knowledge?

"If this conflicts with your experience, the burden is on me to prove the veracity of my hypothesis. So, I will share how buyers and vendors affect Lead Time length based on their business practices. Since I will have shown by that time that Cycle Time length cannot effectively drive Lead Time length, I must show what does. I will prove that Lead

Time length is driven by the combined business practices of the buyer and the vendor. I will detail those practices and show how they influence Lead Time length."

"Education then, consists of the buyer and vendor understanding their planning system, understanding Lead Time and Cycle Time, quantifying the effects, costs, and drivers of Lead Time length."

"What does one do with the education?" I asked rhetorically.

"Once we agree that Cycle Times and Lead Times are separate but related we are then free to reduce Lead Time lengths independently of Cycle Time lengths. We can then examine the proposition that inventory (safety stock) compensates for any Lead Time lengths in excess of One Day, the compensation phase" Some heads nodded, some shook.

"For example, do retailers demonstrate this fact by their very existence?" All heads nodded however I saw a big BUT on some faces. I continued, "What the other links in a supply chain need, what we need to do, is to systemically define and control the amount of safety stock that allows us to quote One Day Lead Times. We need to cost effectively emulate the retailers ability to quickly respond to their customers needs. The quantity of safety stock held by a vendor must, by definition, be less than existing inventory quantities in the supply chain. Or there are no cost savings. Therefore, I will show you how to calculate the advantages of One Day Lead Times through the systemic use of empirically defined safety stock quantities strategically placed throughout the supply chain. I will show you how to Manage Inventory"

"Oh yeah!" I hear them moaning under their collective breaths, "anyone can drive down Lead Times by increasing their inventories, right now the last thing we need to do is increase inventory levels. Hang on and have faith" I reply,

"If I do not prove to you that you will have less inventory when you reduce Lead Times then you can criticize me. Remember I said I will show you how to manage inventory, I did not say I will show you how to increase inventory."

"The first technique allows a vendor to use the inventory levels created by the business practices of its organization to lower the Lead Time quoted to the next link in the supply chain. It calculates product Cycle Times as a first step in a Lead Time reduction program. The calculation affects the determination of safety stock quantities required at each link in the supply chain."

"The next technique builds on the first by calculating the quantity of finished goods safety stock required to insure buyer satisfaction while quoting a One Day Lead Time. The key to this step is to insure that the planning system recognizes, and uses, safety stock as you and I intended it to be used. I show how existing planning systems view safety stock, the weakness of that view, and how to modify your planning system to effectively use safety stock quantities. The result of these techniques is the ability to effectively quote One Day Lead Times to your customers allowing each of you to reap the cost reductions defined during the education phase. This techniques systemically integrates two links in the supply chain; you and your customers."

"Lastly, I reduce finished goods safety stock quantities by establishing safety stock quantities of raw, or component, materials from vendors who quote Lead Times greater than One Day. The formulations and planning system modifications mirror those of the second technique but I treat them separately due to the time required to build safety stocks from vendors who quote long Lead Times. This technique allows a business to reap the increased cost savings that result from the reduction finished goods safety stock needed to support One Day quoted Lead Times. It systemically integrates your vendors into your planning system forming a fully integrated supply chain"

"I finish with a review of what I have shown and a method for sharing that allows the buyer to share that knowledge with all vendors. I place the onus on the buyer because any vendor can, and in my view should, apply the techniques independently. The buyer needs to address those vendors who, for whatever reason, do not independently reduce their quoted Lead Times to One Day."

"Lastly I address management. One may integrate their supply chain by insuring effective communication between links, but communications, in and of itself, does not reduce inventory and lower costs. Each link in a supply chain will not react as you want it to. As you strive for full supply chain integration, your planning systems must be able to compensate for those vendors who cannot, or will not, react as you want (at least until you can find replacements). The way to accomplish that task is to insure that communications effectively affects the planning systems and insures that the planning systems can adapt quickly to every changing business conditions. In short you must manage lead times which means, in the world of One Day Lead Times, you must systemically manage inventory."

"What I will share is not theory. I have used these techniques in the real world. I instituted these techniques in an organization whose sales were about $50,000,000 annually. The results included a $10,000,000 reduction in buyer inventory levels and a 50% reduction in transactional costs (three planners were no longer required). When I retired, the folks remaining were in the process of reducing raw material inventories by half ($5,000,000). However, those numbers are only history, my history, I share them just to give you an idea of the savings available to you. You will calculate your potential savings with me as we go through the process. Once you decide to implement

One Day Lead Times it takes just three months to start reaping the benefits. That means that after three months you will have freed up additional resources needed to begin Cycle Time reduction programs that will add savings in cost, improve quality, and further reduce inventory levels."

"Let us begin our journey."

Chapter 1

WHY LEAD TIMES EXIST

"OK, let's start with the center, the cause, the reason why Lead Times exist in the first place – the Planning System. What do you think of when you hear the term planning system?" As the answers came, I wrote them on a flip chart."

**Computers
Bills of Materials
Operations sequence
Formal plan
Time
MRP
Direction**

And the obligatory "Master of us all", which got its equally obligatory chuckle.

"Right, I said" as I filled the page. "It's all of that and more."

"The area I'm concerned with today is how the planning systems functions relative to time sequencing. Not just the sequencing of manufacturing operations, but the sequencing of all actions that consume time. Modern computer based planning systems started with GANTT charts developed during World War II. Non-repetitive planning systems used PERT charts developed later by the Navy for the Polaris submarine project. These systems used time as the prime factor in planning. They tracked actual consumed time against the planning time to show how the plan was progressing. This diagram represents a planning system for the purpose of our discussion.

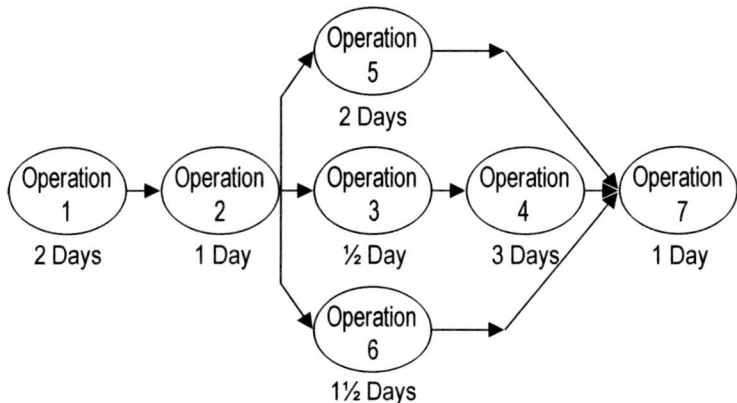

The time elements are the Lead Times for each specific operation."

A hand shoots up.

"Yes" I ask?

"Don't you mean the Cycle Times for those operations?"

Thank God, there's one in every class.

"Tom, excellent question, please reassure the rest of the group that you are not a plant, that I have not paid you in advance for setting me up with such a great question. First, how many of you agree with the thrust of Tom's question, that the times used by the planning system are Cycle Times."

There is some hesitation but about two-thirds of the class raised their hands.

"OK, thanks.

"In this graphic, I mean Lead Times. Why Lead Time and not Cycle Time is one of the key points that influences everything I'm going to be covering, but to understand the relationship between Lead Time and Cycle Time I need to establish a foundation. That is what I am attempting to do right now, establish the foundation. Shortly I'll be back to the relationship and spend some time building on that."

"OK" Tom replied, "I just want to be clear, my planning system uses Cycle Times for operations and Lead Times for Bills of Materials."

I said: "I understand your point, but please, for now anyhow, let me continue to call the time elements Lead Time, because the planning system really doesn't care if the time elements are Lead Time or Cycle Time. The system is a number cruncher; it doesn't care where the numbers come from, or even if the numbers are accurate. It only wants numbers to crunch. The judgment about the validity of the numbers is yours and mine, the people who input the numbers into the planning system."

"OK" let's continue. "The point of this graphic is to show how planning systems use the time assigned to each element. You see, understanding how planning systems use time is basic to understanding why this class exists, (why my book exists)."

"The planning systems automatically use the times allocated to each operation to predict and to direct actions."

Predict:

"The planning system calculates the critical path of the flow to determine the completion day of Operation 7 when given a start date of Operation 1. It sees the path as Operation 1+2+3+4+7 or 7½ days after the start of Operation 1. Or it may, given any start date, calculate the end date of any, or all, subsequent operations."

Direct:

"The planning system calculates the start date of each operation based on the desired completion date of Operation 7. When the planning system directs actions it does not allow slack time, rather it directs the latest possible date for an action to begin. So *Start Dates* (SD) added to our graphic looks like this:"

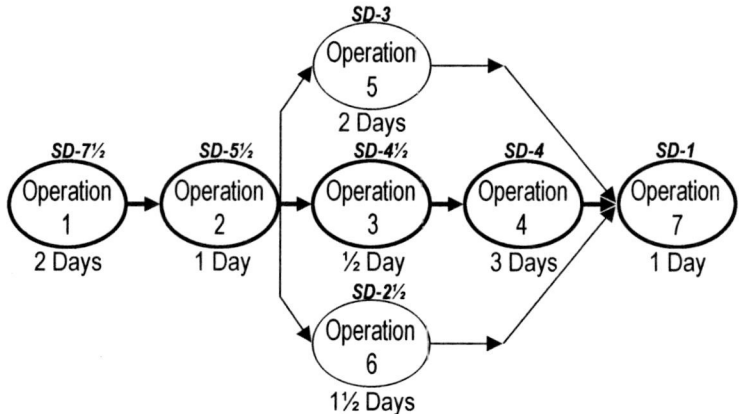

"As you look at the graphic, think of your own situation, i.e. your planning system, your work area. Doesn't this make sense? If Operations 5, and 6 were Lead Times for materials needed by Operation 7, the planning system would not direct you to order the material three and one-half days before they were needed (critical path). No, the planning system tells you to order the materials 2 days and 1 ½ days before the start of Operation 7 respectively. The importance of the graphic will become clearer as we get into the criteria of Lead Time. Right now I only need your agreement that the graphic fairly represents your planning enviroment (albeit a simple representation)."

"Agreed? I looked at the group trying to read the body language, "Will somebody repeat back to me what I have just said."

"OK" said the Betty seated at my right, "one of a planning systems functions is to use time to calulate the start or finish times of all activities that support a specific outcome given a desired start or finish time."

"Beautiful" I replied, "I could not have summarized it better. Thank you."

"Now, here is my last point about Lead Time lengths. Who provides the numbers? Lets say Operation 5 is procuring a necessary component. Who provides the 2-day Lead Time entered into the planning system?"

Kathy raised her hand, "Yes" I nodded.

"The vendor who supplies component." she said.

"Excellent, now let's say Operation 2 is a sub-assembly operation done in house. Who provides the 1 day Lead Time used by the planning system?" I asked.

Kathy continued, "The sub-assembly department based on their Cycle Time"

"Great," I said. "But remember, at this time we are not concerned with how the number is derived only in who provided the number."

"From our examination, we develop the definition of Lead Time. Lead Time is the amount of time, defined by the vendor, required to meet a request of demand. Does anyone have a problem with that definition?"

Bill answered for the group, "with the caveat that we need to discuss how the number is calculated, or arrived at, I guess I can accept that definition"

Looking around the room, I saw general agreement. This meant that either they agreed, or they acquiesced. In either case, I was not facing open rebellion. That might come later, but for now, they were willing to give me the benefit of the doubt.

"Once we agree to a premise, I will build on that agreement. If I do my job correctly, each segment I present will build on the previous and lead to the next."

Plowing on, I said "Accepting that definition, implies that Lead Time values must meet certain criteria or the effectiveness of the planning system is put at risk. Next I'll define those criteria and justify them?"

❖

❖

❖

Chapter 2

LEAD TIME CRITERIA

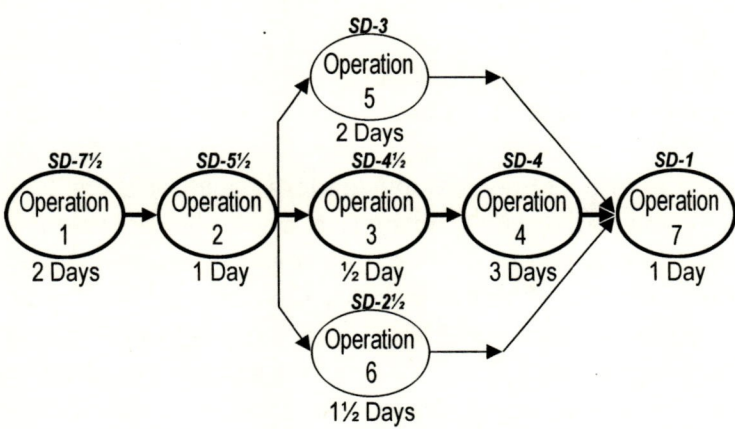

I took the planning system graphic over to a sidewall and taped it up where all could see with only a little inconvenience.

Next, I hung up the definition of Lead Time.

Lead Time is the amount of time, defined by the vendor, required to meet a request or demand.

"The planning system uses the time values defined as Lead Time and, adds and/or subtracts them from defined dates to predict or direct actions. For the planning system to function properly and, for our businesses to operate effectively, each Lead Times entered into the planning must be credible, adhered to, and timely." I pointed to the graphic again. "Assume for a second that the times represented here did meet those criteria, what would happen? Let's take Credible first."

Credible or accurate "By this I mean that all parties believe the Lead Times in the planning system to be true. They believe the output of the planning system to be accurate."

"To demonstrate, I'll talk about myself."

"There was a time in my professional life when I insisted that any Lead Time in my planning system reflect a worst case scenario. I knew that my vendors could react inside the Lead Time entered into the system, but I thought I needed a longer time to insure that no matter what was asked of me, I could respond. To further justify the longer Lead Times, I added the fact that my ability to react inside Lead Time told my management that I was a good negotiator. I realized that Lead Times that were not credible served my self-interest. I know that none of you would think that way, that's why I use myself as a worse case example."

"Vendors inflate Lead Times for the same reasons. When a vendor cannot (or will not) react inside a quoted Lead Time the buyer labels that vendor as inflexible. The vendor, in order to show their willingness to serve, inflate Lead Times to give themselves room for improvement. What did this thought process cost? Easily violated quoted Lead Times costs the vendor credibility with the buyer. The buyer knows that whatever Lead Time the vendor quotes, it can be bettered. Where is the bottom line? It is an unknown quantity."

"While that's going on the buyer loses credibility with the production planner for the same reasons. Lastly, marketing loses faith in the entire planning system because they know that all they have to do is increase the pressure (noise level) a little and product will be made available to them."

"The planning system is relegated to an advisory role with true product Cycle Time as an unknown. Please understand that most of this occurs on purpose. I said I wanted a Lead Time I could violate for my own selfish reasons. The salesperson I dealt with did the same thing to serve his/her selfish interests. Both of our managers, to serve their self-interest, did the same thing. All of us motivated by the same factor; we were showing that 'we are responsive.' Meanwhile all of us undermined the purpose of a planning system. Without the system doing what it is designed to do, all of us gave up managing and became reactors to events."

"The buyer pressures the vendor to react inside Lead Time to show flexibility. On the other hand, once we violate the Lead Time, it loses credibility. The buyer no longer knows what the real Lead Time is. This lack of information moves up the supply chain and no one knows how quickly the chain can react to change. Without credible Lead Times, marketing becomes optimistic and agrees to sales requests that may not be met by the supporting supply chain. We, buyers and vendors, shoot ourselves in the foot when we easily violate our quoted Lead Times *(This argues for One Day Lead Times where there would be no temptation to request quicker reactions, but I get ahead of myself)*."

"Now I want to get off the soap box and ask what do you do. What you think about the need for the credibility of Lead Times in your planning system?"

Bill, one of the purchasing managers started the conversation. "You miss the point Dave, the planning system needs repeatable information not frozen information. Buyers and vendors work in the normal day to day environment without asking that stated Lead Times be violated. The key to your argument revolves around the ability of a vendor to consistently react quickly to the buyer's demand. Lord knows I will not allow my buyers to sign onto extra liability to insure short Lead Times. The vendor must reduce Cycle Times to the point that One Day Lead Times become a reality. The buyer must maintain pressure on the vendor to reduce Cycle Times. Lead Time reduction will follow if the buyer is performing his or her job. Short of that, the buyer must use whatever means, short of accepting contractual financial liability, to insure that vendors quote the shortest possible Lead Times."

"Thanks Bill, you have summed up what this course is all about" I said "My problem is that to fully respond to your comments means I would have to leave the foundation I am trying to establish. Therefore, I ask this favor. Would you allow me to answer you in small segments that tie in the way I present this material?"

"Certainly" Bill responded, "carry on."

"OK here's what I want to do. I'm going to post Bills comments on the wall, as I proceed I will attempt to tie what I say to Bills comments, when I'm done, we may disagree but I want the disagreement to be based on the facts I present. Is that acceptable to everyone?"

I tore a sheet from the presentation pad and taped it to the sidewall. On it I wrote:

---

1. **The planning system requires repeatable data.**
2. **The planning system does not require frozen data.**
3. **Normal operations do not force buyers or vendors to violate Lead Times.**
4. **Vendors must be able to meet customer's demands.**
5. **That vendor's ability to react must not be the result of inventory for which the buyer is liable.**
6. **The key to vendor responsiveness lies in their ability to reduce Cycle Times.**

"Is that a fair representation of you comments Bill?" I asked.

"It's OK for now" Bill responded.

"Any other comments" I asked. I looked around the room, most seemed focused on what Bill had said. I continued.

"The point I was making is that for the planning system to function effectively, that is for the planning system to effectively plan, the Lead Times entered into it must be credible. When I used Lead Times that I knew were worst case I said to anyone using the planning system, use the Lead Time if you want but if you need quicker response, I can do that for you. I effectively said, 'This Lead Time is a guide, if you want to know what I really can do call me.' Now I suggest the key question we want to ask ourselves is: Is my planning system a management tool or is it a guide?"

Hands went up, I pointed to Tom.

"Planning systems have been, and always will be tools, used to guide people in their decision making process.' He said.

Heads nodded across the room; there was general agreement.

"Remember I said that each element of course would build on previous statements" I responded, "Well this is one of the basic building blocks. In the world we are used to you are correct. The planning system can only be a guide as long as the data it uses is not credible. But, my friends, what would you say if the Lead Times were all one day. What would happen then?"

Again I searched their faces, some nodded, and some were skeptical.

"Look" I continued, "If Bill's point number one is valid, the planning system requires repeatable data, and I agree that his point is valid, then we, who enter the data, must insure that we provide data that can be repeated time and again. We've all been through quality classes and know that quality means every time right. When we input Lead Times that we know can be improved upon we input poor quality data. We know that the only Lead Time that someone will never ask us to beat is one day. How we do that systemically needs to be developed, but that does not change the fact that the Lead Times entered into our planning system must be accurate. Agreed?"

No one took exception so I walked over to the list and in red next to point 1 and wrote, "AGREED"

Karen raised her hand, "Write if it can be supported" she said.

I responded, "Karen, if I get through all 6 points that should support the first right?"

"Ok" she said.

I continued. "If we agree that the data must be accurate then it follows that the data must also be adhered to."

Adhered to "Once you enter an accurate Lead Time into the planning system, managing that Lead Time becomes a challenge that grows proportionally with the Lead Time length. One Day Lead Times require no management because customers do not ask for significant changes during the short term. Changes mean open order maintenance costs (transactional costs). The amount varies based on the actual work required running the gamut from clerical efforts to production interruptions. However, we have all been called upon to process changes. The results, violation of attribute one, credibility, and increased cost based on the practices of the vendor. This is how it works. A vendor who wishes to maintain the credibility of a Lead Time length must demonstrate that an extra ordinary set of actions takes place each time there is an expedite. Those actions include, but are not limited to:" I wrote as I talked.

- **Premium charges for raw materials (violation of another vendor's Lead Time length) and/or,**
- **Overtime charges to produce out of preset planned production sequence and/or,**
- **Exceptional transportation charges (reduction in transportation Cycle Time).**

"The result is 'Dammed if you do and Dammed if you don't.' React inside Lead Time without charge and the vendor shows flexibility and loses credibility. React inside

Lead Time with additional charges and the vendor builds credibility and is perceived as less flexible."

Bill raised his hand. "That's not fair!" he said. "When I ask my vendors to react to my needs, I do not think of it as undermining my planning system. In fact, it's just the opposite; I'm supporting the planning system by providing what's needed when it's needed. And my vendors and my buyers better be able to react to change, that's what I'm paying them for."

"Your last statement is partially correct Bill" I replied. "Your buyers and your vendor need to be highly flexible, but that's not the issue here. What I'm addressing here is the Lead Times loaded into your planning system, not the flexibility of anyone. I'm suggesting that Lead Time length defines flexibility. We should not define flexibility as the ability to react to change by beating the system. Rather, we should define flexibility as a systemic way of operating our business to accommodate a world of change. What I'm stating is that there are two ways of looking at the same issue. There is systemic flexibility and reactive flexibility. Beating Lead Times loaded into the planning system is reactive flexibility, providing short Lead Times is systemic flexibility. I'm not talking right or wrong, I am talking about which is the more effective way of running our business." I continued.

Timely "Credibility and adherence usually relate to Lead Times that can be improved upon. The timely criteria usually relates to Lead Times that are changed without prior notice. Vendors most often violate this criterion because of their method of determining Lead Time length; i.e. calculating Lead Time based on Cycle Time length. When capacity becomes constrained, Cycle Times increase because one of the elements in the Cycle Time length calculation is the queue times between manufacturing operations. As the capacity of an operation fills, the queue time increases for the following orders. Capacity constraints and its effects

Managing Inventory • 15

on Lead Time is the subject for later (Chapter 7), for now I will concentrate on the criteria. Few events cause more frustration than reacting to the planning system's request for action and finding out the data was out of date. The system directed me to place an order. I called the vendor to fill the demand and was told that the Lead Time had increased. At the very least, I had to scramble to meet the demand from another source. In the worst case, my customer's buyer had to be told that we would be late meeting demand. When vendors change Lead Times at order placement time customers:" I wrote the consequences on a chart.

- **Lose faith in the system (credibility).**
- **Find other sources.**
- **Report on an unreliable source.**
- **Design vendors out of their product now or in the future.**

"Vendors who increase Lead Times at the time orders are placed effectively neuter their customers buyers planning system because that system provides out of date instructions to the user. In addition, the buyer's inventories are increased as other materials, purchased to meet the planned need date are received, and sit waiting the pacing material's receipt. Production schedules change, and production priorities change, all in an effort to try to compensate for a Lead Time that changed at the time of need. Timely Lead Times are Lead Times that never change at the time of an actual need. The planning system must have timely data."

"Now" I said walking over to Bill's list, "Lets relate what I have said to Bill's second point: The system does not require frozen data."

"Let's look at this from two points of view, current paradigm, and the One Day Lead Times Process. To survive, let alone flourish as professionals, buyers, vendors, planners, and production managers must be responsive to changing customer needs. That is inarguable. The question before us is not the need to be responsive but the how to be responsive. One method I will call extra-systemically, the other is systemically. Our current paradigm is to act extra-systemically, to rely on the negotiating skills of individual links in a supply chain to better previous commitments. Or worse, to have individual links second guess the other links by providing exaggerated commitments."

"Alternatively, One Day Lead Times, supported systemically, provide the flexibility that Bill and his peers seek while maintaining the integrity of the planning system. Remember my opening slide, *'Imagine what your professional life would be like if all Lead Time lengths were One Day?'* That means that forecast accuracy, frozen or not, is a non-issue when vendors quote One Day Lead Time. I am going to write 'true but they do require data that is credible, adhered to, and timely' next to Bill's point two (2); 'the planning system does not require frozen data'. I want your comments but only as they relate to what has been said. I realize I am asking for a great deal of faith from you that I can deliver a systemic approach to One Day Lead Times, but that discussion will come later."

Nothing! "OK let me ask this. Do you agree that if a planning system is to fulfill its charter effectively, the data it uses must be credible, adhered to and timely?"

"Theoretically yes, but practically no" said Tom. I'll hold to that until you get through the rest of Bill's points."

I looked around and said "Fair enough. Let's proceed."

"We know that Lead Times are data used by a planning system to direct or predict actions. We know that the planning systems needs Lead Times that are credible, adhered to, and timely. Yet, we have not lived this knowledge. We are like the boss who says, 'I don't care what the system says, I will tell you when I want it, you tell me how much it will cost.' Why do some of us insist that we can manage better than the planning systems we hired to do that portion of our job? It's not the planning system we have a problem with; it's the fact that our customers demand quicker responsiveness than the planning system says we can provide. Said another way, we can't respond effectively to changing customer demands with the current Lead Time lengths. Our problem is the Lead Time lengths that we enter into our planning systems, which we know we can beat given enough motivation. The system is doing what it is designed to do. We do what we feel we have to do to meet customer needs even if that means we have to override the information we entered into the planning system in the first place. We respond to customers effectively with One Day Lead Times. We respond to customers ineffectively with longer than One Day"

"OK, we know what Lead Times are, the amount of time, defined by a vendor required to meet a request of demand."

I pointed to the definition on the chart paper that hung next to Bill's six questions as I said: "We know that for our planning systems to function properly that the Lead Times we enter into the planning system must be credible, adhered to and timely."

"Now that we know about Lead Times let's look at Cycle Time."

❖

❖

❖

Chapter 3

CYCLE TIME

"*Cycle Time* is the sum of actual or allocated times necessary to complete an operation or process." After I wrote this on chart paper, I placed it next to the definition of Lead Time.

Lead Time is the amount of time, defined by the vendor, required to meet a request or demand.

Cycle Time is the sum of actual or allocated times necessary to complete an operation or process.

"How is this different from Lead Time?" I asked rhetorically. "The simplest way to distinguish them is to look at how they are derived. The vendor assigns Lead Time, whereas Cycle Time is the sum of its component elements. Let me give you an example. A finished product's Cycle Time is made up of the sum of as many sub-products Cycle Times and/or Lead Times as necessary to complete the product. Just as the cost of a finished product contains a number of elements, Cycle Time is made up of individual operations/processes. Process mapping identifies elements of cost and/or time. A typical product process map might look like this:"

Process	Operation	Time Elements	Cost Elements
Product	Receive an order	Cycle Time	Labor
	Load order into internal systems	Cycle Time	Labor
	Order raw material	Cycle Time	Labor
	Vendor *Lead Time*	Lead Time	Material
	Receive raw materials	Cycle Time	Labor
	Release for manufacturing	Cycle Time	Labor
	Manufacture	Cycle Time	Labor
	Ship to customer	Cycle Time	Labor
	Total	Cycle + Lead Time	Labor + Material

"The total time is the sum of the Cycle Times from the mapping process plus the Lead Time quoted by the vendor. *Cycle Time* is the sum of actual or allocated times necessary to complete an operation or process."

"Does anyone have a problem with what I am saying?" I asked.

Bill led off for the group again. "Vendors define Lead Time just as you define Cycle Time. They list their process elements just as you did, and the sum of those elements defines their Lead Time, so I don't see where you're going here. Lead Time and Cycle Time are the same things, or at least Cycle Time defines Lead Time."

"Bill, you are right, some vendors do as you state, but not all. For example, does your group ever buy hardware, you know, screws, bolts, etc."

"Sure" he answered.

"What is the Lead Time for hardware?" I asked.

"Nothing" he said, "but that's different, those items are manufactured in bulk and kept in stock."

"My only point is that while some items may have a Lead Times that its vendor justifies by detailing their Cycle Time elements, others do not. I'm going to get into this in more detail after our break, but we must understand that Cycle Time and Lead Time are different. If they were the same,

Managing Inventory • 21

they would always be the same, but since we just identified an example of where they are not (hardware), I'll say they are different. Right now, barring any other comments, I'll continue to address Cycle Time. OK?"

Bill wasn't happy but he let me continue.

"Cycle Time process maps for each operation within a product Cycle Time further identify time and cost elements. For example, this map details one element of the previous process map, Receive order."

Process	Operation	Time Element	Cost Element
Receive order	Answer phone	Cycle Time	Labor
	Record data (request)	Cycle Time	Labor
	Determine if request can be met	Cycle Time	Labor
	Inform customer	Cycle Time	Labor
	Record firm order	Cycle Time	Labor
	Total	Sum of Cycle Times	Sum of Labor Costs

"In one of my previous lives, as an Industrial Engineer, I timed and analyzed individual operations continuously looking for improvement opportunities. Likewise, process mapping continues to detail member operations into smaller and smaller segments for analysis. Therefore when one refers to a Cycle Time one must be specific in stating the process associated with the Cycle Time."

"My last assignment was supporting a printed circuit board assembly department whose Cycle Time was 2 days. That Cycle Time was only the assembly of a board, the total product Cycle Time for an assembly averaged one hundred and fifty (150) days. Product Cycle Time was made up of 148 days procurement Cycle Time and 2 days assembly Cycle Time. Each of these is further broken into its components. The 2 day assembly Cycle Time was made up of ½ day parts kiting time, ½ days actual assembly, ½ day test and ½ day ship Cycle Time. Each of these can be further broken down into value added and non-value added steps."

"Cycle Time reduction programs concentrate on the elimination of the need for non-value added elements of a process. The many publications on Cycle Time Reduction already available make anything more I might add redundant. Suffice to say; Cycle Time processes are actually a whole series of processes. Each of the sub-processes in each of the processes has cost, quality, and inventory associated with it. That means that each sub-process and each process presents an opportunity for improvement. That is the reason why Cycle Time reduction programs are so important and cannot be minimized. A brief review of the assembly Cycle Time reinforces my point."

Element	Cost	Quality	Inventory
Kiting	Bill of Material creation, Systems support, necessary documentation, parts storage equipment, direct labor to pick parts to match Bill of Material, all materials.	Bill of Material accuracy, Inventory count accuracy, Inventory part accuracy, and correct selection of parts to match the Bill of materials.	All parts that make up the Bill of Material.
Assembly	Kiting plus direct labor.	Assembly and parts accuracy.	Bill of Material plus kiting costs.
Test	Assembly plus direct labor.	Assembly plus test program, nests and operation.	Assembly plus testing costs.
Ship	Storage space, shipping containers and labeling, direct labor to ship, transportation.	Correct labeling and shipping instructions.	Total cost of product.

"This table is not intended to be all inclusive, but rather, an indication of the level of complexity involved in a relatively simple analysis of a clear cut operation. Costs, quality concerns, and inventory costs grow, through each element of each process. The sum of the processes defines total costs, quality and inventory levels for a process or product. Cycle Time defines cost, quality, and, inventory quantities. Cycle Time reduction *is the key* to improved quality, reduced costs and inventory reduction."

"Let us look at another reason why Cycle Time is not entered into a planning system, while Lead Time is."

"In the example given above I stated that the 2 day assembly Cycle Time was made up of ½ day parts kiting time, ½ days actual assembly, ½ day test and ½ day ship Cycle Time. That is not accurate. Our planning system recorded those times as Cycle Times but the actual time consumed by each operation varied. Planning system times are not the same as process mapped times (actual times). Actual Cycle Time varies based on lot sizes, backlog and numerous other factors, just as actual costs vary around some plan. Look again at a process map."

Process	Operation	Cost Element	Time Element	Variation
Populate Board	Kit parts.	Labor	Cycle Time	Part location and containerization
	Set up auto-insertion machine	Labor	Cycle Time	Previous set-up and part containerization
	Load bare boards	Labor	Cycle Time	Containerization
	Run board	Labor	Cycle Time	Board and part quality
	Remove and inspect	Labor	Cycle Time	Set-up, board and part quality
	Total	Sum of Labor costs	Sum of Cycle Times	Variation around planned

"Each element has a time and cost associated with it. Each time and cost element assumes certain conditions as true, i.e. parts are in the proper container, in the proper quantity. Real life does not always follow our assumptions. Sometimes two partial containers provide the proper quantity instead on one full container. That fact affects actual cost and time yet we cost and plan based on pre-assigned conditions."

"The times entered into the planning system were the time values provided by the kitting area, the assembly area, and the test area. They were really Lead Times. They allow for process variation and queuing problems."

"OK, I'm going to take a break here, but so that you have something to think about while you're getting coffee remember." Under the definition of Cycle Time, I posted its purpose.

The purpose of Cycle Time is to define a benchmark, a starting place, from which to make improvements in costs and quality in processes.

Concluding "Just as we continually challenge costs, so also, we continually challenge Cycle Times."

Under the definition of Lead Time I posted its purpose.

The purpose of Lead Times values, in a planning system, is to define when an action needs to be taken so that a result will occur when desired or they calculate when a dependent action can start.

"The vendor defines Lead Times values. The process defines Cycle Time. Cycle Time and Lead Time are related but are neither synonymous nor interdependent. Since that is the case why are so many of us convinced that Cycle Time drives Lead Time?"

"See you in 15 minutes."

❖

❖

❖

Chapter 4

HOW WE GOT HERE OR,

WHEN WE DO WHAT WE DID,

WE GET WHAT WE GOT

Back from break I started.

"I said I was going to get back to the subject of Cycle Time vs. Lead Time. I'm back. In fact, I'm going to spend a considerable amount of time discussing with you the relationship between Cycle Time and Lead Time. I cannot stress strongly enough the importance of these concepts relative to all that follows. So please interrupt me as often as you need to until you understand what I am talking about. Disagree if you care to, but I need you to give me the assurance that I have made my point clearly. The burden of this communication is on me, not on you, so keep me honest."

"If what I share is accurate, then what we have been doing, and how we have been doing it, needs to be challenged. The facts I am sharing force us to look at the world differently than we have previously."

"Before our break I gave you the definition and use of Lead Time and Cycle Time. I said that Lead Time is the amount of time, defined by a vendor, needed to respond to a request or demand. Planning systems use Lead Time to direct or predict actions. I further stated that for Lead Times to do what they are designed to do they must be credible, adhered to and timely."

I pointed again to my posters, "Cycle Time is the amount of time taken or allocated to complete a process. Cycle Time provides the starting point for improvements in costs, quality, and inventory through the elimination of the need for non-value adding activities within a process. Cycle Time and Lead Time are related but Cycle Time does not drive Lead Time. We tend to think they do but they do not. Understanding their relationship is what I am going to spend the next hour addressing."

"I'll start by addressing, in greater detail why we do not force our Lead Times to be credible, adhered to, and timely. I stated that perceived self interest is one of the reasons we have for allowing the Lead Times we enter into our planning systems to be neither, credible, adhered to, nor timely. Another reason is that it seems so logical. We believe Cycle Times, that vary, drive Lead Times. Our life experiences support our logic. Our personal planning system uses Lead Time as a guide not as a constant. Our natural tendency is to do the same thing in business as we do in our personal lives. What our life experiences have taught us seems most effective."

"As a demonstration I want you to recreate your own planning system. A planning system uses time as a controller."

"This morning you had to be in this conference room at 7:30 AM. You set your alarm clock to a specific time, based on that need. List the time elements and values you used to figure out what time you needed to wake up. Your headings are: Action" I wrote on the flip chart as I spoke.

"Next note the time allotted, CT for Cycle Time, LT for Lead Time, and lastly the rationale you used to define the times allotted. Then summarize as I have, Arrival Time less total actions equals Wake up Time."

My next two slides guided the class through their assignment.

Action	Time allotted	CT	LT	Rationale
Total				

Arrival Time _____
less Total Actions equals Wake up time _____

"In each space note:"

_____

1. "Actions you used to determine the time the alarm was set for.
2. The time allotted for each action.
3. Define the time element as Cycle Time (CT) or Lead Time (LT), or both.
4. Why you think of that element as Cycle Time or Lead Time (or maybe both)."

_____

I allowed three minutes and continued.

"If you're done set that sheet aside for a minute, if not continue filling out your sheet, while I relate my story."

"My education on Lead Time and Cycle Time started as soon as I learned to plan based on expected times, and continues today. When did I start planning? Four experiences come to mind. See if you can relate to these."

As I spoke, I listed the four experiences on the chart paper with the headings.

**Doctor's appointment
Paper route
Dry Cleaning
Grocery shopping**

Doctor's appointment: "The first dealt with planning an appointment with the doctor. I had to be at the office at a certain time. The planning process consisted of estimating the time elements of the steps needed to get where I had to go. The steps included dressing properly and, travel from home to the doctor's office. My parents ran the planning system and monitored progress. 'Hurry or we'll miss the bus.' Converting the system to the same worksheet you used yields:"

Action	Time allocation
Dress properly	20 minutes
Travel	30 minutes
Total	50 minutes

Goal time
less Total Actions
equals Start up time   50 minutes

"An example, delivering morning papers. It took me forty minutes to deliver my morning papers. An extra large basket on my bike allowed me to improve delivery time because I didn't need to stop and switch bags from my cart, or sled, to the handlebars of my bike. I used Cycle Time in my planning system I used it to calculate the time to set the alarm clock to based on the time I needed to finish the route. Reducing the Cycle Time meant I could sleep in longer" I followed with:

"Next if I needed a suit cleaned and pressed by a certain date, I took it to the dry cleaners one week earlier. I did not run this planning system, the dry cleaner did. I used the time in my planning system but its value was set by the dry cleaner. If my planning system balked at the value, (I needed the suit in three days instead of a week) I had to pay a premium to change its value."

"Lastly if I needed a loaf of bread I went to the supermarket and purchased it. I balanced the quantity of bread that I bought against the inconvenience of walking to the store and the life expectancy of the bread. Bread is always available on demand."

"These examples follow the same logic you used in your chart. They reinforce my previous conclusion that Lead Time must be credible, adhered to and timely. Your planning system depends on the relative accuracy of the time estimates you used. Guess wrong, or more likely, something unexpected happens, say a traffic jam, and you are late. What we have learned is that when elements of time, used in planning, are inaccurate, our plan suffers. We may be early, or late, but the fact remains that disturbing the time elements affects the expected outcome."

"We learned that Cycle Time drives Lead Time. When we ran into a delay, our Cycle Time increased. An increased Cycle Time meant that we had to allow more Lead Time if we expected to meet whatever the goal was. We learned that of the two options, early is better than late. Slack (excess time) in Lead Time length is better than not enough time (being late). Therefore, we normally allow some slack in our Lead Time so that we are never late. Said another way, Cycle Time plus slack (allowance for the unforeseen) equals Lead Time."

Under the time calculation heading for the doctor's appointment and paper route I wrote

Lead Time = Cycle Time + slack

I reiterated; "Cycle Time drives Lead Time"

"Ok so far?" I asked. Heads nodded, Bill smiled, I continued.

"In the third example, dry cleaning, I learned that Cycle Time might not drive Lead Time. Lead Time is a variable and negotiable. I know that I can pay a premium and get the suit cleaned in a day. Does this conflict with my training? Compare that fact with my paper route example. I affected elapsed time (Cycle Time) with a bigger basket on the bike. I changed the work content. With the dry cleaner, I did not affect work content (cleaning is cleaning), but I was able to affect Lead Time. This result appears to contradict the conclusion I made earlier; namely, that Cycle Time drives Lead Time. But, when I thought about it, I realized that what the dry cleaner did was change the slack allowance built into the Lead Time. The Cycle Time did not change: Lead Time did, because my job was expedited through the process. It reinforces the concept that Lead Time cannot be less than Cycle Time."

Next to dry cleaner I wrote

Lead Time = Cycle Time + slack, but slack can be a variable.

"Lastly I went to the store for bread. I ignored bread making Cycle Time and used as Cycle Time the time consumed in travel to and from the store. Lead Time for bread is less than the bread making Cycle Time. The Lead Time for bread is equal to travel Cycle Time. No conflict exists here; rather one just has to decide which Cycle Time to use when calculating Lead Time. If inventory exists, manufacturing Cycle Time can be ignored."

Next to grocery shopping, I wrote

Lead Time = 0 when inventory exists

"My learning (training) is complete. I know that:" I return to the chart paper.

- **Lead Time is based on Cycle Time.**
- **Lead Time is defined for me. It starts when I make a request and ends when that request is satisfied. Lead Time is simply Cycle Time plus slack, used to plan.**
- **To be safe, Lead Time should contain some slack (be inflated) to compensate for the unforeseen.**
- **When inventory exists, the Cycle Time used to generate the inventory does not count in the Lead Time calculation.**

"I bring these facts from my personal experiences into the work place. I know about Cycle Time, I know about Lead Time. They are roughly the same thing said a different way. I know about planning."

"Still Ok," I asked?

"So far so good" was the general response.

"The problem'" I continued, "is that Lead Times used in a business planning system must be credible, adhered to, and timely. Our personal planning Lead Times are:" I checked off the following.

- **Inflated to try to cover for the unforeseen (inaccurate).**
- **Can be changed as needed (not adhered to).**
- **Need little warning when change occurs (not timely)."**

"In our business environment, *Cycle Time* is the sum of actual or allocated times necessary to complete an operation or process. The suit was the unit of work, cleaning and pressing its major components whose time values, added together, equal the Cycle Time."

"*Lead Time* is the amount of time, specified by a vendor (the dry cleaner), that elapses from the time a buyer expresses a desire until that desire is satisfied."

A hand went up. "Mary?" I said.

"You keep saying that Lead Times must be accurate, adhered to and timely, but you have yet to present the case as to why that is true. From your examples, as long as the time allocated is at least long enough there is no problem."

Ted joined in "I see what can happen when Lead Time changes without warning, but I agree with Mary on the rest. What's the problem as long as we can consistently meet the Lead Time entered into our planning system?"

"An important point" I acknowledged. "The simple answer is that as Lead Time length increases, costs increase for the buyer and the vendor, but I need to develop that more. For now I'll add the concern to the list started by Bill."

Adding to Bill's list I wrote:

What are the effects of Lead Time length?

"Does that capture your concerns?" I looked at Mary, who nodded. Ted showed agreement and the rest of the class did not object. I continued.

"Lead Time and Cycle Time appear to us to be the same because we have experienced the ability to change both. We unconsciously mix them as part of our normal life. When the boss gives us an assignment that we know will take two hours (Cycle Time), we do not quote the boss a two hour Lead Time. We increase the time based on our current backlog (the same as allowing extra time to drive to work in case of a traffic jam). If we need supplies to do the job assigned, we need to add the amount of time to get the supplies to our process time then allow for our backlog. The result is our quoted Lead Time. Notice that, except for those dealing directly with a consumer, we are both buyer and vendor. We use Lead Time quoted to us, add our Cycle Time, add an allowance for capacity (backlog), and then quote a Lead Time to our customer. Look at the chart you made above. Did you mark down Cycle Times, or did you include some allowance on top of the actual Cycle Time. Would you risk being late some mornings because you did not include an allowance for the unforeseen?"

"Another business fact is that when Cycle Time is changed, the buyer does not necessarily see the change. The buyer always sees a change in Lead Time. When a manufacturer, who sells through a distributor, or to keep with my example, when a bread manufacturer reduces Cycle Time the buyer, does not see the reduction because their needs have always been satisfied from inventory."

"I purchased electronic components from stocking distributors. When the manufacturer reduced Cycle Time, it was invisible to me. I also bought from manufacturers. When a manufacturer changed from a make-to-order strategy to a make-to-stock strategy (adds inventory), I saw the Lead Time reduction. Assuming no process improvements (Cycle Time did not change) I still saw a Lead Time reduction. These distinctions do not occur in our personal lives."

"I related some history about Lead Times and Cycle Times, doctor's appointment, paper route, dry cleaners and a trip to buy bread. Now look again at the form you made out. Which items are Cycle Times? Which items are Lead Times? The problem we run into is that we don't know the difference based on personal experience."

"Again:" I pointed to the charts.

"In business, *Cycle Time* is the sum of actual or allocated times necessary to complete an operation or process."

"*Lead Time* is the amount of time, specified by a vendor that elapses from the moment a buyer expresses a desire until that desire is satisfied."

"Said another way, Cycle Time is process driven, Lead Time is a business decision. The point is that we need to filter our life experiences in light of our professional knowledge of time. We need to consciously differentiate between Cycle Time and Lead Time. Why? In our personal lives, the cost effects of time changes are miniscule compared to the cost effects of time changes in business. Businesses that receive inventory early have the cost of that inventory to carry. Late receipts cost businesses in terms of the changes to production schedules, carrying costs of all other materials and customer relations."

"The Lead Times we use in our business planning system are not credible, adhered to, or timely because too many of us believe that it serves our self-interest to have flexible Lead Times. Our personal experiences support the view that Lead Time and Cycle Time are two ways of saying the same thing. These factors frustrate the purpose of Lead Time (to direct action or predict results in a formal planning system) and our planning system ends unable to effectively direct or predict. We, of course, blame the system. Besides, when we maintain discipline in a formal planning system our careers and egos suffer. When the boss wants something done in a hurry, we receive rewards when we beat the system. The problem is not the system; the problem is Lead Time length. If quoted Lead Times were shorter we would seek our rewards elsewhere, say cost and price, and the planning system would work as it has been designed to."

"We know why we do what we do, lets look, in more detail at Cycle Time and Lead Time."

❖

❖

❖

Chapter 5

CYCLE TIME VS. LEAD TIME

Continuing our discussion on the distinction between Cycle Time and Lead Time I said.

"Lead Times and Cycle Times are two separate entities. The terms are not synonymous. They are not interchangeable. To do so is the equivalent of using the terms cost and price interchangeably. They are driven by different factors, and used for different purposes."

"Cost is the result of activities. Each activity adds a dollar amount to a product or process, to define the total cost. Allocated costs (example: overhead) make up a part of the total but each element of cost is identifiable."

"The marketplace sets the selling price. The difference between cost and price is profit. One may address cost elements to increase the profit margin or to lower costs to meet a market supportable price, but the cost does not always drive the price."

"Virtually all manufacturing follows the same steps. While cost models add all elements, time models count only the longest of simultaneous time elements together. Granted the length of time each step takes will vary with each product. From this, we can see that the products total Cycle Time is the sum of the sequence of process Cycle Times and the longest component vendor Lead Time."

"Lead Time is the amount of time that elapses from the time a buyer expresses a desire until that desire is satisfied. Said another way; Lead Time is the amount of time one waits for another to respond. Individual Lead Times may overlap as when several items are purchased to produce a product. Each item has a Lead Time, but what defines a product's Cycle time is the longest Lead Time associated with the product. Remember in the discussion of Cycle Time I pointed out that certain operations could be done simultaneously; well the same is true with Lead Time."

"In both cases, when the total is calculated, the longest of the simultaneous operations is the only one counted. Remember the planning system I started with?" I pointed to the chart highlighting operations 5 & 6 vs. 3 plus 4.

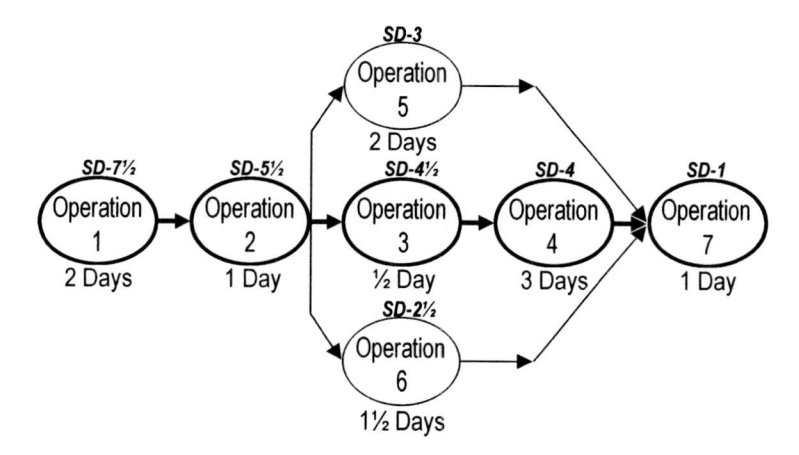

```
                            SD-3
                         Operation
                             5
                          2 Days
  SD-7½         SD-5½     SD-4½      SD-4        SD-1
Operation →  Operation → Operation → Operation → Operation
    1            2           3           4           7
  2 Days        1 Day      ½ Day      3 Days       1 Day
                            SD-2½
                         Operation
                             6
                         1½ Days
```

"Lets put Costs, Cycle Times, and Lead Times on the same table." I put on another slide on the projector.

Operation	Cost element	Cycle Time element	Lead Time element
1 Purchase	Labor + Material	Purchase Cycle Time + Vendor Cycle Time	Purchase Lead Time + Vendor quoted Lead Time
2 Sub assembly	Labor	Process Cycle Time	Sub assemblers Lead Time
3 Purchase	Labor + Material	Purchase Cycle Time + Vendor Cycle Time	Purchase Lead Time + Vendor quoted Lead Time
4 Sub assembly	Labor	Process Cycle Time	Sub assemblers quoted Lead Time
5 Purchase	Labor + Material	Purchase Cycle Time + Vendor Cycle Time	Purchase Cycle Time + Vendor quoted Lead Time
6 Purchase	Labor + Material	Purchase Cycle Time + Vendor Cycle Time	Purchase Cycle Time + Vendor quoted Lead Time
7 Final Assembly	Labor	Process Cycle Time	Final Assembly quoted Lead Time
Total	All Labor + all Material	All Cycle Times	Product Cycle Time = sum of Lead Times of operations 1+2+3+4+7

"But this still begs the question, how does each step define the Lead Time it will quote to the next link in its supply chain. You or I want to buy an item. We place an order; the vendor receives the order, fills the order, and provides the product. The element 'fills the order' is the variable that the vendor defines. That element controls the Lead Time for the item we buy. The vendor always defines the Lead Time, because the vendor determines how to fill an order. The vendor's choices range from fill the order from available inventory to start manufacturing upon receipt of a buyer order."

"The following charts show Cycle Time and Lead Time in the steps of a sample supply chain. All operations at each link in the supply chain shown have been grouped into four steps: Order Materials, Vendor Lead Time, Build, and Shipping. This chain consists of four links – a raw material vendor, a sub-assembler, a final assembler, and finally a consumer." As I worked through the slides, I continued.

Raw Material				Sub Assembly				Final Assembly				Consumer
O R D E R	W A I T	B U I L D	S H I P	O R D E R	W A I T	B U I L D	S H I P	O R D E R	W A I T	B U I L D	S H I P	Order and receive finished product

"The first link in this supply chain is a raw material vendor. The raw material vendor gets raw material for their process. So I do not sound like a cheer leader (raw, raw material) I will designate the starting material as core material. The process map for Raw Material manufacturing is:"

Raw Material Vendor			
Order Core Material	Vendor Lead Time	Manufacturing Cycle Time	Ship
2 days	40 days	5 days	1 day

As I looked around the room, I asked "What is the product Cycle Time for this Raw Material Vendor?" They just looked at me. "Come on I joked, this is not intended to embarrass anyone, just give me your best guess." A couple of mumbled answers and then I heard "48 days."

"Ok" I said "good answer."

A new slide, I continued, "As we did in our personal planning system example, we calculate the Raw Material product Cycle Time by adding its elements. Order core materials, plus vendor quoted Lead Time, plus build, plus ship equals total Cycle Time. The Cycle Time for this Raw Material vendor is:

Total Cycle Time is the sum of all activities (2 + 40 + 5 + 1) = 48 Days

"The Total Cycle Time is made up of three Cycle Times (Order, Build, Ship) and one (the longest) vendor quoted Lead Time. Now my next question is; what is this Raw Material Vendors quoted Lead Time? This time I will caution you that these are trick questions because there is no correct answer. Rather just an answer that matches this problem. With that as a preamble give me your best guess as to the Lead Time here."

Again, there was caution throughout the room. Finally, I heard, "60 days," followed by, "48 days."

I replied, "This Raw Material vendor believes that Cycle Time drives Lead Time and therefore quotes the next link (Sub Assembly Vendor) a 48 days Lead Time. Put it altogether on one table, the product time profile for the Raw Material Vendor is:"

Raw Material Vendor			
Order Core Material	Vendor Lead Time	Build Cycle Time	Ship
2 days	40 days	5 days	1 day
Total Cycle Time is the sum of all activities (2 + 40 + 5 + 1) 48 Days			
Lead Time is set by the Vendor			
This raw material Vendor quotes 48 Days Lead Time			

"The next link in the supply chain is the Sub Assembly vendor who orders and receives raw materials from the first link in the supply chain. Like each link in this chain the purchasing Cycle Time is 2 days, Build Cycle Time is 5 days, and Pack and Ship Cycle Time is 2 days. The raw material quoted Lead Time is 48 days as shown above. The total product Cycle Time process map for the Sub Assembler is:"

Sub Assembly Vendor			
Order Raw Material	Raw Material Lead Time	Build Cycle Time	Ship
2 days	48 days	5 days	1 day

"Again" I asked, "What is the Sub Assembly product Cycle Time?" The responses were louder this time "56 Days." "Correct," I said, "we calculate the Cycle Time by adding the elements. Order raw materials, plus raw material Lead Time, plus build, plus ship equals total Cycle Time. The Cycle Time for this link in our supply chain is:"

**Total Cycle Time is the sum of all activities
(2 + 48 + 5 + 1) = 56 Days**

"Before I ask you what the quoted Lead Time is I must let you in on a few facts. This Sub Assembler has been in negotiations with the their buyer, the Final Assembler (me). The goal of the Final Assembler has been a reduction in Lead Time quoted by the Sub Assembler. In fact," I added, "the sub assembler has been told that unless the quoted Lead Time is significantly reduced I will find another sub assembler that I can work with. With that background what Lead Time do you think the sub assembler quoted?"

Again, I heard voices, "10 days, 5 days," and one voice suggested "1 day."

"All are correct," I said, "but since I made up this slide in advance I will use 6 days. On the other hand, I might say that due to the skill of the buyer, and the cooperation of the vendor, the Lead Time quoted by the Sub Assembly Vendor is *6 days*. How? Inventory. The Sub Assembler agreed to maintain a stock of Finished Goods in order to quote the 6 day Lead Time. Distributors, and the entire retail industry, quote short Lead Times because they carry inventory. Put it altogether on one table, the product time profile for the Sub Assembly Vendor is:"

Sub Assembly Vendor			
Order Core Material	Raw Material Lead Time	Build Cycle Time	Ship
2 days	48 days	5 days	1 day
Total Cycle Time is the sum of all activities (2 + 48 + 5 + 1)			
56 Days			
Lead Time is set by the Vendor			
The Sub Assembler quotes 6 Days Lead Time			

"The next link in this supply chain is the final assembler. Its total product Cycle Time process map is:"

Final Assembly			
Order Sub Assemblies	Sub Assembler Lead Time	Build Cycle Time	Ship
2 days	6 days	5 days	1 day

"Now what is the Final assembly Cycle Time?" The entire group was with the program now and replied "14 days." "Correct, you're getting good at this," I said. "Again we calculate the Cycle Time by adding the elements. Order Sub-Assemblies, plus Sub-Assemblers Lead Time (the Sub Assembler Vendor quoted 6 days Lead Time above), plus build, plus ship equals total Cycle Time. The Cycle Time for the Final Assembly vendor is:"

**Total Cycle Time is the sum
of all activities
(2 + 6 + 5 + 1) = 14 Days**

"Note first, that the Cycle Time at the Final Assembler is low due to the low Sub Assemblers Lead Time. The Cycle Time is a mere 14 days. Hence a new law:"

I hung a new chart next to the definitions of Lead Time and Cycle Time.

"A Lead Time reduction anywhere in a supply chain is a Cycle Time reduction at the next Link in that chain."

"I have another story for you," I started.

"The Final Assembler (me) has not missed a promised delivery date in 50 years. That's right, 50 years. With that as background tell me what Lead Time the Final Assembler quotes?"

I received more than my fair share of skeptical looks. What was I driving at? Bob broke the ice. "Ok never late! I say you quote 30 days Lead Time."

"You got it" I replied, "Well almost anyway. I quote 20 days. Now, for our sake, tell us your thought process Bob."

He smiled "Well never late, you must throw some fat into your Lead Time to cover for the unforeseen."

"Again you're right on," I continued. "The Final Assembler wants to protect against the possibility of something going wrong. This Final Assembler also wants to manage a business where an active backlog of orders exists. The Final Assembler decides that all these goals will be met by quoting the buyer a *20 day* Lead Time. Put it altogether on one table, the product time profile for the Final Assembler is:"

Final Assembly			
Order Sub Assembly	Sub Assembly Lead Time	Build Cycle Time	Ship
2 days	6 days	5 days	1 day
Total Cycle Time is the sum of all activities (2 + 6 + 5 + 1)			
14 Days			
Lead Time is set by the Vendor			
The Final Assembler quotes 20 Days Lead Time			

"Put all product's Cycle Time profiles together to show the profile for the entire supply chain (I'll abbreviate to save space on the paper):"

Raw Material Vendor				Sub Assembly				Final Assembly				Consumer
ORDER	WAIT	BUILD	SHIP	ORDER	WAIT	BUILD	SHIP	ORDER	WAIT	BUILD	SHIP	Order and receive Finished Product
2	40	5	1	2	48	5	1	2	6	5	1	
Cycle Time is 48 Days				Cycle Time is 56 Days				Cycle Time is 14 Days				
Lead Time quoted is 48 Days				Lead Time quoted is 6 Days				Lead Time quoted is 20 Days				Lead Time is 20 Days

"Several facts emerge as this last chart is examined." I pointed to the appropriate spots on the chart and said:

- "Lead Time can be equal to, greater than, or less than Cycle Time *(The effects of these Lead Time decisions will be detailed in the next chapter)."*
- "In a multi level supply chain a product's Total Cycle Time is hidden because:"
- "Each link in a supply chain can only see the Lead Time of the previous link."
- "Quoted Lead Time becomes an element in the next links' product Cycle Time."
- "The vendor always defines Lead Time length (a buyer can negotiate but the vendor makes the business decision)."
- "A Lead Time reduction anywhere in the supply chain is a Cycle Time reduction at the next link."
- "Cycle Time length is always defined by the process."
- "Each link's product Cycle Time is the sum of its process Cycle Times and the longest Vendor quoted Lead Time."

I continued, "Cycle Time is to Lead Time as Cost is to Price, they are related but one does not drive the other. At its simplest level, the delta between cost and price is profit. At its simplest level, the delta between Cycle Time and Lead Time is supply chain inventory quantities (higher costs) and/or responsiveness to buyer needs. When Lead Time is longer than Cycle Time, inventory is located at the buyer's location and the vendor cannot react quickly to changing buyer needs. When Lead Time is shorter than Cycle Time, inventory is located at the vendors and responsiveness increases. To keep the analogy going, Cycle Time and costs are always going to exist. The goal is to minimize, or control both. The generator of successful Cycle Time reduction sees the advantage of lower costs, increased quality, and lower inventories. That is why Cycle Time reduction programs are important. Said another way; the effects of long Cycle Times are higher cost, poorer quality, and higher inventories. Lead Times are a separate issue. The effects of Lead Time drive the need for One Day Lead Time length."

"OK?" I asked.

"You just proved my point." Bill stated. "If each vendor were to reduce their Cycle Time, then the next link in your supply chain could, if they negotiated properly, receive a Lead Time reduction. It's also true that they should see a price reduction because as Cycle Times are reduced, costs are reduced. The buyer should share in those reductions."

"Hang in there Bill, I'm almost there." I replied. "For now do you agree with the comparison I am making, that is that Cycle Times are to Lead Times as cost is to price?"

"I will if you agree that, just as the key to increased profits is cost reduction, the key to Lead Time reduction is Cycle Time reduction." Bill challenged.

The rest of the class was following this exchange and from the looks I was getting they were convinced that Bill made a valid point.

"Don't misinterpret what I am saying Bill. Cycle Time reductions are extremely important and must be pursued. What I just showed was that Lead Time length can be a separate issue, addressed independently, and accomplished much more quickly than Cycle Time reduction programs. Cycle Time reductions are the results of continuous improvements, whereas Lead Times length can, and should, be reduced to one day quickly independently of Cycle Time reduction programs. The delta between cost and price is profit. In order to increase profits one must either increase prices or reduce costs. The delta between Cycle Time length and Lead Time length is inventory. To explain further we need to examine the effects of Lead Time length relative to Cycle Time length. The only exception to this rule is custom or one of-a-kind goods. Notice that the vendors who supply this class of goods do not have a material planning system like repetitive manufacturing vendors have. A less dynamic material planning system lessens the need for Lead Times that meet the criteria I pointed out earlier. Therefore, the advantages gained through One Day Lead Times are less. Not gone, but less. It is still to every ones advantage to reduce the Lead Time component of Cycle Time in order to reduce costs and inventory levels."

Chapter 6

THE EFFECTS OF LEAD TIME LENGTHS

"The supply chain I shared earlier showed that vendors justify their quoted Lead Time lengths based on their view of their world. That is, that each vendor rationalizes quoted Lead Time length to each buyer. Factors used to justify quoted Lead Time length are." I listed the following:

1. **Cycle Time drives Lead Time,**
2. **Capacity drives Lead Time,**
3. **Vendor business practices drive Lead Time, and**
4. **Buyer's practices drive Lead Time.**

"Now we know that Lead Time has criteria; Lead Times must be credible, adhered to and timely. Given that fact, the question is; which of these factors meets these Lead Time criteria and yields the lowest additional cost? Or, as Mary asked, what are the effects of Lead Time length?"

"First I will look at Cycle Time and Lead Time. Next, I will look at what happens when capacity drives Lead Time length. Then I look at vendor business practices, and lastly I examine how buying practices affect Lead Time length."

"Remember the basis for effectiveness:"

- "Lead Times must be credible, adhered to and timely and"
- "The longer the Lead Time the greater the cost to both buyer and vendor (The next chapter address how to measure those costs)."

"As we saw earlier, relative to Cycle Time, Lead Times can be equal to, greater than, and less than, the Cycle Time of the manufacturer. Can this be true, and if so, what are the effects?"

1. *Lead Time equal to Cycle Time.*

"The ideal option is to have Cycle Times so low that product is produced and available as the buyer states a need. The ideal is not an option, first because the manufacturer, most often, does not control demand. Demand is infinitely variable while, short of zero Cycle Time, supply can not be infinitely variable. Second, product Cycle Time includes vendor Lead Times. That means that the entire supply chain, for the product, must have product Cycle Times so low that all consumer demands are satisfied when expressed. If possible at all, it would take years to implement. It is like saying the ideal is to have zero cost, that is not going to happen. What we strive for is to drive Cycle Time and costs as low as possible. We strive to continuously improve."

"Wait just a minute," said Bill. "Are you trying to tell us that the Toyota Just In Time system does not work? That JIT is a myth?"

"Excellent point Bill. No way will I say that Cycle Time reduction efforts have failed. I am suggesting an add-on to those systems, a way to reap some benefits quickly while freeing up resources to work on Cycle Time reduction. Let me ask you, Bill how long did it take Toyota to get its system working effectively?"

Managing Inventory • 53

"Years" replied Bill.

"And how many companies are you aware of that pervert Just In Time systems into Jammed in Trailers, JIT?" I continued.

Bill smiled.

"The points I'm making are:"

1. "The ultimate answer to cost, and inventory reduction with improved quality is Cycle Time reduction."
2. "Cycle Time reduction does not, necessary translate into Lead Time reduction *that is the point I am making now*."
3. "Your customers do not have to wait for Cycle Time reduction in order to reap the benefits of Lead Time reduction."
4. "No one can achieve One Day Lead Times unless they truly understand the drivers of Lead Time."

"Remember, the raw material vendor calculated quoted Lead Time length based on Cycle Time."

Raw Material Vendor			
Order Core Material	Vendor Lead Time	Manufacturing Cycle Time	Ship
2 days	40 days	5 days	1 day
Total Cycle Time is the sum of all activities (2 + 40 + 5 + 1) 48 Days			
Lead Time is set by the Vendor This raw material Vendor quotes 48 Days Lead Time			

"Let's follow an incoming order to see the real world."

> "Single product manufacturer."

- "Assume that the vendor has been in business for some time and has an existing operation."
- "Assume further that a single product can be produced at a maximum rate of one hundred (100) units per day due to capacity constraints."

"First, order entry personnel add the order received to the existing open order backlog. If the new total backlog exceeds 4800 units (100/day max. capacity * 48 days Lead Time) the promise date will not be met without the increased cost of overtime (NOTE: the 4800 total is simplistic! Balanced Input/Output with input equal to out put and no inventory requires that buyer need dates must line up with the 100 per day capability. At the very least buyer needs could not exceed 100 on any given day.)."

"The sales office must monitor active backlogs to insure that the quoted 48 day Lead Time will be met. There is no Win; if backlog is under 4800, excess capacity exists which adds to unit cost or the vendor quotes shorter Lead Times. If the Lead Time is shortened, then the Lead Time is not credible, is not adhered to, and must be calculated at the time of order receipt. The buyers planning system has been neutered."

Managing Inventory • 55

➢ "Lets switch to a manufacturer of multiple products."

"First, order entry personnel add the order received to existing open order backlog the same as above. The new total backlog varies as the Cycle Times of various products consume available capacity. This leads to work overload in the sales office as they try to monitor incoming orders and backlog (if not the sales office then production planning). Lastly, the vendor neuters the buyers planning system again by quoting variable Lead Times."

"When Cycle Time is used to calculate Lead Times, the results vary as capacity is consumed."

"The only cases where Cycle Time can drive Lead Time are:"

- "When the vendor has infinite capacity at no cost and zero Cycle Times, or"
- "The demand rate is *always* less than the available capacity and the vendor absorbs the resultant costs (reduce profits)."

"An analogy might be a fast food business. Warming trays allow short Lead Times as long as demand stays stable and under capacity. But let a bus pull in and Lead Times increase. Let there be a slow period and either the quality of the food decreases (that may be redundant), or food must be scrapped due to the amount of time in the warming tray."

"Business planning systems are more complex and the results of variable Lead Times expand with that complexity. Production change requests (expedites, de-expedites, and cancellations) from sales, marketing, or management force production planners to determine what jobs to do in what order, on a daily basis. This in turn forces the vendor to bypass the planning system and determine their production requirements as a series of reactions to the pressures of the moment. Therefore, their buyers cannot consistently predict Lead Times from their vendors. The buyers feel they must protect themselves with safety stock. The label of unreliability stigmatizes the vendor."

"The retailer, whose vendor quotes Lead Time based on Cycle Times, in order to insure product availability, overstocks that vendor's item. This reduces the variety of product available to consumers at the retailer as inventory consumes available space."

"When long Lead Time and Cycle Time exist, the vendor and buyer suffer the effects of long Cycle Times (increased costs, inventory, and lower quality). The effects detailed above, combined with the effects of long Lead Time, are detriments to all concerned."

I set up a slide that read:

Conclusion:

Quoted Lead Time lengths set to equal Cycle Time lengths force the vendor to violate Lead Time criteria as capacity constraints and conflicting production priorities yield variable quoted Lead Times.

Managing Inventory • 57

The hands went up all around the room. I picked one, "What about lean factories, those who have adopted the Toyota planning system, all I have read states that they successfully reduce Cycle Times and quote Lead Times based on short Cycle Times."

"I can't address that entire topic right now because I have more ground work to lay, but as a teaser I'll point out several facts" I said

1. "A kanban is an inventory, that is where kanbans exist the goal is to limit inventory based on Cycle Times. A manufacturing unit receives a signal to build based on the fact that their Cycle Time is equal to or less than the amount of time it takes to consume the kanban quantity at the next manufacturing link. So buyer Lead Times match the last step Cycle Time not the product Cycle Time. When demand exceeds capacity either Lead Time increased or demand is controlled by supply."
2. "As you read those examples note that buyer Lead Time is set at the time an order is taken. Said another way, the Lead Time quoted does not feed a planning system. Where vendors have been trained to react either JIT or quickly, the Lead Time quoted is one day or less. That is exactly where I'm going. The difference is that I show how to get there very quickly, less than 3 months, where getting all links in a supply chain into one day Lead Time lengths, as quoted in the books, takes five years or more."
3. "Lastly, do not interpret anything I'm saying as a criticism of short Cycle Times or lean manufacturing. The key to cost control, inventory control and quality control lies in Cycle Time reduction. The methods I show shield the buyer from the current world

while each of us works to improve that world. My goal is to compensate for long Cycle Times while minimizing costs and freeing up those forced to react to changing buyer needs so they can work on reducing Cycle Times."

"So, as I pointed out earlier about Bill's point number 6, 'the key to vendor responsiveness lies in Cycle Time reduction' I say a resounding YES. *BUT* I am not saying that Cycle Times drive Lead Times, I am saying that Cycle Times defines the amount of inventory required to support a quoted Lead Time. I then ask how you intend to get there quickly considering the twin facts that most of us spend most of our time reacting to planning systems and our vendor base is huge. That my friends is what this class is all about, but to get there we need the foundation I'm laying right now."

2. *Quoted Lead Times longer than Cycle Times.*

"The vendor who quotes Lead Times longer than Cycle Times, typically, is the one the buyer knows they can negotiate with and expedite. In short, the buyer does not believe this vendor's Lead Time. Not meeting that Lead Time criterion alone disqualifies this option, and the effects of long Lead Times add to the problem. The result: a Lead Time with no credibility resulting in added inventories, and higher transactional costs for the buyer and the vendor."

"Why then do some vendors continue to quote Lead Times that are longer than their Cycle Times?"

"The answer; they believe that they are protecting themselves from the vagaries of the marketplace, and supporting price/profit objectives. They base their logic on life experiences that have shown them that scarcity is good for business. Let's face it; collectibles grow in value as supply decreases. So, they reason that the same logic holds true for other items, i.e. as supply drops, price increases. Add to that the apparent fact that an active backlog leads to better production scheduling and vendors naturally lean toward longer quoted Lead Times."

"Tom Peters recommended we 'Under-promise, Over-deliver' (*Thriving on Chaos*, Alfred A Kroft, 1987) which is the same logic. Beating promises makes buyers happy. The error in the logic, as applied by those who quote long Lead Times, is that Lead Time, in a supply chain, requires credible, accurate and timely information. Consumers may be happy when you meet their needs quicker than they were led to believe but any link in a supply chain that uses a planning system gets added costs as the reward. An early delivery means excess inventory (an early receipt is inventory until all materials required are received). The planning system tries to coordinate all material receipts to be available when needed. That coordination is frustrated as promised materials are delivered early and sit as excess inventory until the remaining items on the bill of materials arrive when scheduled."

I replace the last slide with:

Conclusion:

Quoted Lead Time set greater than Cycle Time violate Lead Time criteria as vendors and buyers violate quoted Lead Times to meet needs.

---

3. *Lead Times shorter than Cycle Time*

"I love short Lead Times so, as a general rule, I argue in favor of very short Lead Times. The most effective way to accomplish this however is with inventory at the vendor's location. But, isn't there too much inventory already? How much inventory should be kept? How does the planning system react to the inventory? Who assumes the risk associated with the inventory?"

"However, a systemically controlled quantity of inventory does have certain advantages."

"At one time we had fruit cellars stocked with canned fruit and vegetables (inventory). If you ran out, the Lead Time was next summer. Today, almost all fruits and vegetables are available year round. The Lead Time is effectively zero. A supply chain works the same way. As One Day Lead Times becomes the norm, costs and inventory levels decrease and buyer responsiveness increases. Again, please consider the fact that most of the retail industry lives this truth."

"Holding inventory allows vendors to compensate for varying demand from their customer base. Each buyer consumes at a different rate and each vendors quoted Lead Time defines the inventory levels that those buyers need to protect their consumption rate. As an example let us look at a vendor who quotes a one week Lead Time. The rate of consumption forecast is 100/week, and the stocking strategy is 8 weeks."

I put up the slide.

Supply Chain Inventory
(Manufacturer quotes One Day Lead Time)

Wk. #	Made	Buyer East			Buyer Middle			Buyer West			Chain
		Bought	Sold	Inv	Bought	Sold	Inv	Bought	Sold	Inv	Inv
1	5000	800	100	700	800	80	720	800	90	710	4730
2			120	980		70	1050		80	1030	4460
3			110	870		90	960		85	945	4175
4			140	730		100	860		102	843	3833
5			110	620		60	800		75	768	3588
6			125	495		75	725		80	688	3308
7			150	345		90	635		62	626	3006
8			135	210		80	545		66	560	2725
9			110	100		95	450		65	495	2455
11		980	120	960		80	370		70	425	2185
12			120	840		80	290		65	360	1920
13			115	725		75	215		68	300	1662
14			110	615		80	135		70	235	1402
15			115	500		70	75		72	165	1145
16			110	390		65	10		65	100	905
17			100	290	635	70	575		70	30	665

"The vendor manufactures in lot sizes of 5000. When Lead Times are low, initial order quantities can be lower. The vendor chooses the manufacturing strategy based on whatever factors the vendor chooses. But the vendor keeps the inventory. This gives the vendor the ability to average demand based on actual usage. When the vendor keeps the inventory, that inventory satisfies the varying rates of consumption. Reorders are filled from inventory and the potential quantity of product returned is reduced. The links in a supply chain previous to the retailer gain more because of the reduction in transactional activity based on open orders."

I put up the last slide.

"For now I think we can agree that, under the correct circumstances, One Day Lead Times pay."

Conclusion:

Quoted Lead Times set lower than Cycle Time meet Lead Time criteria while allowing greater buyer service and lower transactional costs, but at the cost of inventory. The costs of keeping empirically defined and systemically controlled quantities of inventory at the vendors location is offset by the reduction in transactional costs, the reduction in the total amount of inventory in the supply chain, and the elimination of the costs associated with phantom demand changes. One Day Lead Times pay.

Chapter 7

QUANTIFYING THE EFFECTS
OF LEAD TIME LENGTH

"I'm going to quantify Bill's points 3 and 7 next." I started.

"Why do I care about Lead Time length? As long as I know the length, and load it into my planning system (personal or business), I can react as I need, right? I know that the purpose of Lead Time is to direct when an action needs to take place to drive an expected result. Since I know the Lead Time, I know when I need to take action. That is, I know when to set my alarm clock in the morning. I know when to place a purchase order. I know when I need to release a manufacturing order to production. As long as the Lead Time is credible, accurate, and timely, I should be happy. But, we know we are not happy with long Lead Times. Why?"

I listed the items on the chart as I said, "Because as Lead Time length increases:"

- ❖ **Costs increase (Each of these cost can be quantified and tracked).**
    - ➤ **Increased transactional activities**
    - ➤ **Increased inventories**
    - ➤ **Production planning disruptions**
- ❖ **Inventories increase**
- ❖ **Customer service decreases for all parties affected, and**
- ❖ **Vendor's effectiveness decreases.**

Lead Time and Time

"At the risk of offending anyone who believes I have a remarkable grasp of the obvious, a primer is in order. What follows is necessary because, if it were understood and acted upon, this course would not be needed. All quoted Lead Times would be one day or less."

"As Lead Time length increases the buyer must look further into the future to determine buy quantities (demand). The further into the future we look the greater the probability that things will change between now and then. How do we see into the future? We make an educated guess based on what we know at the time we look. Some of us have computer models to help us, but in the end, it is, at best, an educated guess."

"Does anyone disagree with that statement?"

No one raised his or her hand.

"Use you neighborhood shopping mall as an example. When the actual demand is less than guessed, retailers are forced down one of two roads depending on their contractual relationship with their vendors: have sales (lessen profits), or return unsold product to their vendors for credit (reduce the vendors profit). The vendors, OEM's, see a drastic reduction in demand as the retailer attempts to reduce inventories or they have excess inventory. When the demand exceeds forecast, prices (profits) may rise, or buyers are lost to competitive products due to lack of supply. The closer, in time, actual demand is to forecasted demand the better. Many of us call this forecast accuracy. Most of us complain about forecast accuracy. We fail to recognize that, based on the data available at the time we made the forecast it was accurate. The problem is Lead Time length, not forecast accuracy. We know that we modify forecasts as time progresses. Let's face it; what we really want is a frozen forecast; not increased forecast accuracy. That won't happen."

Forecast Accuracy

I put up a new slide.

"Lead Time length directly affects how actual demand will vary from forecasted demand like an expanding cone of sound. The further from the origin the greater the area it covers. Starting at zero, the effect of zero Lead Time, the expanding area of the cone represents the magnitude of the effect as the Lead Time length increases."

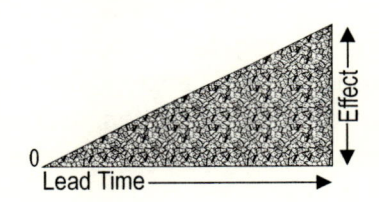

"True, Lead Time length effects are not as mathematically symmetrical as the graphic suggests, but our experiences validate the fact that they do increase as Lead Time increases. If the entire supply chain were willing to wait to have their needs satisfied, Lead Time would cause no problems other than the wait. Since the ultimate buyer (the consumer) must be satisfied on demand, those who supply their needs are required to forecast demand in order to create the shortest possible Lead Time (exceptions exist where consumers are willing to wait and to pay, but they are few)."

"Now, forecasts are needed because the actual time a supply chain needs to react to a demand normally exceeds the amount of time the buyer is willing to wait. For example, how long are you willing to wait for a pair of socks? How long does it take the entire supply chain to manufacture a pair of socks? Would you wait that long?"

A hand went up. "Yes?" I asked Bill.

"I don't see a problem, I don't sell socks. I took a survey of our customers and found that most are willing to wait 3 months for our product. Those who wanted it quicker were willing to pay extra, so for me it is a win-win situation."

"Again thanks for leading me into the effects of Lead Time Bill."

Effects of Long Lead Times

"Today we replenish food quickly; the result is that a minimum inventory of food is required. Years ago, this was not the case. I remember a fruit cellar in our home that was loaded with fruits and vegetables that my mother canned each fall. This inventory lasted through the winter. We sought a balance between cost, space, potential spoilage, and buyer (family) satisfaction. The determiner was product availability. Fruit and vegetables were not readily available in the winter, if you wanted them; you had to build an inventory in the summer and fall. We seek a similar balance in businesses today. To achieve that balance businesses need to quantify the effects of Lead Time length." I clicked them off"

- ❖ "*Costs,* which can be further broken down into:"
  - ➢ "*Transactional* Where repetitive manufacturing exists, Lead Time drives transactional activities (costs) in proportion to the Lead Time length. For this example I will say that:"
    - "We update the planning system weekly (the more often we update the system the greater the transactional activity that results)."
    - "The buy policy (stocking strategy) for the item equals thirty days of supply i.e., each delivery quantity meets 30 days of demand."

"We incur transaction costs each time the planning system signals a potential change to an existing open order. A potential change means that the system directs a change.

The vendor may not accept the change, may offer a counter proposal, or may accept. These interactions vary between buyers and vendors based on business conditions and relationships. Regardless of the result the system still directs that an action take place and someone needs to evaluate that suggestion."

"Calculating the potential for changes to open orders then equals, Lead Time divided by planning system update frequency multiplied by the number of open orders. The formulas are:" As I spoke I worked through several slides.

- Determine the number of scheduled deliveries.

$$\text{Scheduled Deliveries} = \frac{\text{Quoted Lead Time}}{\text{Buy policy}} = \frac{150}{30} = 5$$

- Determine the number of times the planning system updates before receiving an open order.

$$\text{System updates} = \frac{\text{Quoted Lead Time}}{\text{Days between system updates}} = \frac{150}{5} = 30$$

Switching slides I then said, "Calculate the number of potential changes to all existing open purchase order delivery schedules between the time of order placement and order receipt and multiply by the cost of each activity."

**Potential change requests =
(# of scheduled deliveries * # of system updates) * cost of activity.
Or
5 * 30 = 150 * $**

"This table shows the effect of converting the above to a Lead Time length vs. Potential changes. Potential changes decrease as Lead Time length decreases."

Lead Time (days)	Scheduled Deliveries	Systems updates	Potential changes to open orders
150	5	30	150
90	3	18	54
30	1	6	6
10	1	2	2
5	1	1	1

"Lead Time length drives transactional activity (costs). When a buyer attempts to change an open order, a vendor must respond to that request. Even if the answer is that the vendor does not agree to the proposed change, someone has to spend time (time is money) answering the request. Therefore, the vendor sets the Lead Time, and the vendor, and the buyer pay in terms of transactional activity."

"Let us assume that the vendor allows no changes inside Lead Time, and the buyer agrees. Does that fact change the transactional activity (costs)? Yes, to the degree that a buyer does not communicate with the vendor. But, the system still directs the buyer to take an action. Planning systems might be filtered to block out messages based on time, but not based on vendor. The bottom line; Lead Time length affects transactional costs for the buyer and the vendor. The average cost per transaction equals the percentage of buyer/vendor activity per week spent on open order maintenance. When 50% of their time is order maintenance, then 50% of their pay is transactional costs. Test this fact in your environment by asking your buyers, salespersons, or yourself 'If all Lead Times were one day, what percentage of your time would be spent on open order maintenance?'"

Managing Inventory • 69

Increased inventories. "Inventory is not free. The physical location (at either the vendors or at the buyers facility) of the inventory has little affect on the cost of inventory. Lead Time lengths drive inventory quantities that must be paid for by someone."

Raw materials: "This is how I calculate additional cost for purchased components. The buy policies (stocking strategies) define the average amount of inventory any buyer carries."

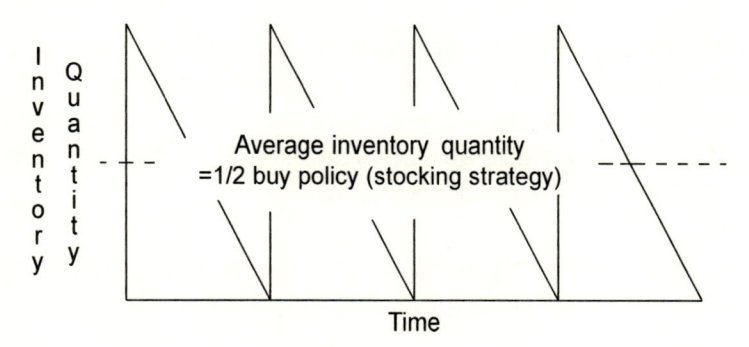

[Figure: Sawtooth graph with "Inventory" / "Quantity" on the Y-axis and "Time" on the X-axis, showing a dashed line labeled "Average inventory quantity = 1/2 buy policy (stocking strategy)"]

When my planning system directs me to purchase quantities equal to thirty (30) days of supply of an item, my average planned inventory for that item equals fifteen days of supply. When I choose to measure along the time line will dictate my inventory level for an individual item. Because the saw tooth is not the same for each item, when I consider all items in a planning system, or all the items an individual buyer is responsible for, time variations cancel each other out. Therefore, the average planned inventory by buyer, or by planning system, equals one-half buy policy. Any organization can measure the inventory cost of Lead Time by subtracting average planned inventory from actual inventory. The delta is the quantity of excess inventory driven by vendor Lead Time."

Planned Inventory Dollars =
½ (buy policy or stocking strategy * Purchase price)
Or
Planning Inventory Turns =
days per year / ½ days of supply per purchase

"The cost of current Lead Times (in terms of excess inventory we carry equals actual inventory – planned inventory)."

"My measurements showed that actual inventory exceeded planned by 2 to 4x (turns were planned at 9.4, actual was 3.5). That represented a considerable opportunity for improvement for an organization that purchased $50,000,000 of materials per year."

- ❖ *Inventory levels at the buyers are a direct result of the Lead Time quoted by the vendor.*

"Inventories increase for each succeeding link in a supply chain that passes on vendor Lead Time lengths as a factor in defining their quoted Lead Time. When the buyer cannot change open purchase orders inside Lead Time, the result is excess inventory, measured in days of supply. Why? When demand declines the quantities due from the vendor will continue for the Lead Time. Another order may not be generated until the inventory is consumed, but the fact remains that the inventory will continue to build to Lead Time. Example: Assume forecast usage of 100 per week. Assume actual usage is 90 per week, buy policy of one week, Lead Time of fifteen weeks."

Managing Inventory • 71

Lead Time & Inventory

Week	1	2	3	4	5	6	7	8	9	10	11	12	13	14	15	16	17
Receipts	100	100	100	100	100	100	100	100	100	100	100	100	100	100	100		30
Forecast use	100	100	100	100	100	100	100	100	100	100	100	100	100	100	100	100	100
Expected inventory	0	0	0	0	0	0	0	0	0	0	0	0	0	0	0	0	0
Actual use	90	90	90	90	90	90	90	90	90	90	90	90	90	90	90	90	90
Actual inventory	10	20	30	40	50	60	70	80	90	100	110	120	130	140	150	60	0

"As you can see, the amount of inventory built up changes as the frozen Lead Time changes. This may seem simplistic because actual usage seldom consistently exceeds or falls below forecast; it varies up and down. So the inventory never gets as large as I indicate, Right? No! All buyers know that it is better to have excess inventory than to shut down a production line due to material shortages. Therefore, buyers protect themselves from the occasions when actual demand exceeds forecasted and the vendor cannot (will not) react. The result is an inventory hedge. The result in terms of inventory is that the numbers shown above actually understate inventory levels directly driven by quoted Lead Times. Define how much higher by using the costs of inventory calculations shown above."

- ❖ Buyer responsiveness
  - ➢ Schedule changes "The example above shows how inventory builds when demand drops. We already know that buyers will protect themselves from the other extreme with hedge inventories. If management adopts a 'No hedge inventory' policy, for whatever reason, buyer responsiveness suffers. Long Lead Times mean that buyers cannot react to changing demand. The inability to react equates to poor buyer performance. A self-defeating (for the buyer) cycle results. Either the buyer carries hedge inventory to insure buyer responsiveness meaning poor buyer performance due to high inventory quantities. Or, buyer responsiveness suffers when demand increases beyond forecast again meaning poor buyer performance."
  - ➢ Engineering changes "When excess inventory exists in purchased components due to quoted Lead Time length, that excess inventory affects

the ability of the buyer to implement change. We know that the measure of buyer responsiveness is not only the speed of reaction to schedule changes; it includes the speed of reaction to design changes. The change may delete a component (scrap the excess inventory and all incoming orders) or change the configuration of a purchased component. Regardless, the vendor with long quoted Lead Times forces the buyer to implement change to match the vendors Lead Time not the buyers needs. As a buyer, this did not sit well with me. It made no difference whether the engineering change was mandatory (affected fit, form, or function) or could be phased in. I as the buyer transferred control of my product design to the vendor because their quoted Lead Times restricted my ability to react effectively to engineering changes"

- ❖ *Vendor's effectiveness decreases* "I have said that the vendor's internal costs increase as the amount of work expended on order maintenance increase. Additionally costs increase throughout the entire supply chain as quoted Lead Time increases. The additional inventory, carried by the buyer, to insure flexibility inside the vendor's quoted Lead Time, grows and shrinks as actual demand changes. The buyer, in an attempt to control the quantity of on-hand inventory, asks the vendor to change delivery amounts and schedules. The transactional activity that this drives enters the vendors planning system. Then the vendor's supply chain is asked to react to those changes. Changes work themselves through the entire supply chain. Production expedites, or de-expedites as necessary. The vendor's ask their vendors to react as these changes work their way along the supply chain."

"Moving back through the entire supply chain, each link adds costs in direct proportion to its quoted Lead Time length (read quantity of open orders subject to change). The total costs could be collected, using the logic defined in (1) above but, I think, if you determine the cost effects of your quoted Lead Time, logic will dictate that the need for further quantification is redundant. Suffice to say, "As quoted Lead Times increase the entire supply chain pays". The vendor defines its own cost effectiveness when it chooses a rationale used to define quoted Lead Time length."

"This means that, even if your customers are willing to accept long Lead Times, the results of those Lead Times add costs to everyone in the supply chain. The worse case occurs when the buyer returns unused inventory to the vendor for credit. The inventory returned existed because of the vendors Lead Time length but both underutilize resources. The buyer temporarily took up valuable space with inventory. When the goods are returned, the vendor eats the costs of returned goods. The vendor then includes those costs as cost of doing business and passes them right back to the buyer. Truly, everyone loses. It is just not a matter of the money, it means that capable people spend too much time chasing the planning system instead to driving their business."

The hand went up. "You just lost me, where do you get the ability to return unused goods to the vendor for full credit?" asked Mary.

"Good question Mary. Some contractual relationships are set up that way. The best example I can give is the publishing industry, but the principles hold true anywhere a buyer has the right to return unsold goods for credit. You see long Lead Times cause increased quantities of open orders as I showed above, now the book stores have the right not only to cancel open orders but to also return unsold goods to the publisher. Why did the bookstore have so much stock? Lead Time. The bookstore has to be prepared in case the book is a big seller. Since the shelf life of a book is short and the bookstore knows that replacement orders take a long time, and since the bookstore knows it can return unsold books it protects itself by hedging just as you protect yourself from change by hedging. As I have asked earlier, how much inventory do you need when you know that reorder time is short?"

"My last point is this. Think of Lead Time the same way you think about costs. Economic Order Quantity (EOQ) logic states that "fixed" costs drive manufacturing lot sizes. Modern production logic tells us that no costs should be accepted as fixed. All costs can, and should be reduced because costs drive the way an organization thinks and acts relative to customer responsiveness, quality, and inventory. If it is true for EOQ's it is true with Lead Time lengths and for the same reasons. All costs must be reduced; all Lead Times must be reduced. The fact of the matter is that of the two, costs and Lead Times, it is much easier to reduce Lead Time lengths as I will prove later."

Bill raised his hand again. "Dave I will agree with you that our vendors must reduce their Lead Times and share the cost savings you defined with us. But, I do not see how that addresses my statement. Our customers are willing to wait and, better yet to pay a premium, to get our product quicker than our quoted Lead Time. We get the advantages of both worlds. We get the time to smooth our production runs because we can aggregate demand and, we can have our vendors reduce their Lead Time based on your logic."

"Bill" I said, "If you believe that our company's competitive advantage is such that a we need not do everything in our power to attract new customers, everything in our power to increase market share, everything in our power to improve our competitive position then you are right. I added nothing to your knowledge base. If, on the other hand, you believe our future is tied to our ability to improve, to go beyond customer expectations then I suggest reducing our Lead Times has real value. My premise is that we need all the improvements in cost, competitive position, market share, and customer relations we can get."

But, setting that aside, I stick with what I have outlined. All links in the supply chain get real, measurable cost advantages from Lead Time reduction. An integrated supply chain, by definition integrates all links. If, or when, you, or I, fail to integrate our customers into the chain we short circuit ourselves in terms of cost control. That means we must systemically manage short Lead Times throughout the entire supply chain. My goal is to get you to agree with me by the end of today. OK?"

Bill smiled, "OK" he said.

"If it's ok with everyone let's move onto another consideration in Lead Time calculations, capacity constraints."

Chapter 8

CAPACITY AND LEAD TIME

"Let's review again."

❖ "Lead Time is the amount of time, defined by a vendor, required to fill a request or demand. It is used by a planning systems to calculate when an action must be taken so that a need will be met, or to determine when an action may be taken based on the completion of preparatory actions."
❖ "Cycle Time is the amount of time required to move a unit through a process."
❖ "In an effective planning system, Cycle Time does not drive Lead Time. "

"Some of you agree with these facts, some of you, based on your experience, have doubts. The experiences that drive the doubts take the form of having had Cycle Time increases result in Lead Time increases. You 'know' from these experiences that Cycle Time drives Lead Time. Right? Sometimes things happen that change Cycle Time. What I'm going to share now is that those occurrences happen because of a capacity constraint. Sometimes capacity becomes consumed as the result of a quality problem that results in rework or replacement, an unplanned equipment shut down."

"Each of us has seen a plan go awry due to capacity problems. The most common, in our personal lives, is on the highway. Construction causes a lane or two to be closed.

The highway capacity drops, our Cycle Time increases and therefore our Lead Time must be changed, i.e. we need to leave for work earlier; we get home later. Even when we take an alternate route our planned Lead Time increases. If you drop a two-hour job on my desk, all things being equal, you will get it when I get to it (backlog plus Cycle Time determines Lead Time). Most all of our life experiences have shown us how capacity affects Lead Time. The fallacies in applying our life experiences to a business planning system are these:"

Life Experience	Business Environment
Lead Time is short.	Longer Lead Times
Single chain of events avoids capacity conflicts.	Multiple uses for capacity leads to increased rearrangement of priorities.
Operation sequence is simple.	Operation flows are complex with many interdependencies that must be managed using a formal planning system.
Planning on the fly can be effective.	Planning on the fly negates the need for a formal planning system. Lead Time must be credible, accurate, and timely.
Consequences of lateness are minimal.	Consequences of lateness are greater (the succeeding operations can not take place without corrective action). Inventories increase, customer service decreases and the business suffers.
Corrective action can take place for the next cycle.	Corrective action takes place at the end of the new Lead Time. Corrective action techniques lead to higher inventories as buyer hedge against a reoccurrence.

Bill raised his hand again.

"I'll agree that those things can happen but, I pay my buyers to insure that they do not happen. The buyer must keep the pressure on the vendor to insure that they meet their commitments."

"That is an approach," I answered, "For it to work consistently several things must happen:"

- "Capacity problems never occur, or"
- "Your buyers overcome problems by applying pressure on the vendor. That means that another customer suffers. I realize that may not be your concern, but the vendor remembers the customers that they can deal with vs. those who attempt to bully them every chance they get. It's the Fram® oil commercial 'Pay me now or pay me later'."

"I prefer to systemically recognize the real world and build a process that allows the vendor and buyer to attain a low cost Win-Win relationship. Let me continue."

"Those times we experienced a Lead Time change, due to a Cycle Time change, in our personal lives, the amount of time consumed by both was very short. The road construction delay that had me set my alarm earlier was, at most, an hour. I measure Lead Times in the workplace in days, more often, in weeks or months. When I arrived at work late, I had to rearrange that mornings' meetings due to the delay vs. a vendor Lead Time change that forced me to rearrange schedules, possibly add overtime, and occasionally contact customers with the bad news of a late shipment. My secretary was able to help straighten out my calendar vs. changes involving, planning, production, purchasing, and customer relations. Since my production facility has finite capacity, when the job they had planned to run couldn't be run, due to a material shortage, they had to shift another job into its time slot so that when the materials did become available they had the capacity to run the original job."

"That rearrangement affected my inventory. I had a completed job done early (inventory and labor), and other inventory sitting around unusable because not all materials that match up are available. Additionally, I had some idea as to when the construction delay would be corrected, the construction completed, vs. not knowing when, if ever, my vendor would return to the old Lead Time. All this is to drive home the point that, what I considered to be equivalent experiences (personal and business related) were anything but equivalent. I am not saying that a Cycle Time problem cannot generate other problems, I am saying that we cannot allow a Cycle Time problem to be reflected in quoted Lead Times."

"In business, not only is a single link's inventory involved but the process is repeated over and over again as Lead Time changes affect each succeeding link in a supply chain. It is up to the vendor to insure that capacity is not a factor when setting their Lead Time. For an illustration of what happens when capacity is a factor in setting Lead Time, I will tell a story. The basics are typical and familiar to you. It is based on fact, although the names are hidden to protect the guilty."

"Widget manufacturing produced the world famous widgets for me at one time. They quoted Lead Time at sixteen weeks. The vendor liked to keep a twelve-week open order backlog, and allowed one week for order entry, two weeks to manufacture and one-week transit time. This vendor, like many, "knew" that Lead Time equals demand (including backlog) divided by throughput (capacity). In this case, the result of the math was a twelve week Lead Time." On the chart I wrote:

$$\text{Lead Time} = \frac{\text{Demand} + \text{Backlog}}{\text{Capacity}} = \frac{200 + 1000}{100} = 12$$

"The vendor had a nice cushion. Well, as life would have it, demand started to creep up. The result of increased demand was that the formula's answer gradually increased until the calculated Lead Time was eighteen weeks. The vendor reacted by increasing quoted Lead Time to twenty weeks. Why? Because of the formula used to calculate Lead Time.

$$\frac{200 + 1600}{100} = 18$$

The vendor saw the demand increasing and compensated by increasing the Lead Time quoted to customers. We have all done this at least one, or two times in our life. It is a normal human reaction. When we see backlog increase, we increase Lead Time (at least we think, until we can determine if the increase is a fluke or a real trend that will require increased capacity). It is an easy way to test the market to see if we can justify the capital expense required for increased capacity."

"Now ladies and gentlemen there are some facts that are universal in application. One of those facts is; the worse thing that can happen to a buyer or planner is to shut down a production line. When the vendor increased the Lead Time to twenty weeks, the buyer's demand did not go away. The buyer had to scramble to somehow meet demand. Now the buyer has just been burned. Burn me once shame on you. Burn me twice, shame on me. The buyer had to protect the client. How? Hedge! The buyer protects against stock outs by placing an order that insures that if this were to happen again, material is available. Buyers protect against supply interruption, in extreme cases, by reserving capacity at vendors. Meanwhile the vendor believes that he/she has control of the situation. The increased Lead Time will allow production to catch up with backlog. The vendor has bought breathing room by increasing quoted Lead Time. Anyhow, what happened in this real life experience?"

"Widget manufacturing saw the increased quantities in demand (total demand equals normal demand plus increased demand plus hedge) ran those numbers through the Lead Time formula, and low and behold, Lead Time had to be increased again. The same phenomenon happened repeatedly; Lead Times increased from 16 weeks to 18 to 26 to 36 to 52 weeks. A post office branch opened just to handle the increased volume of orders and changes. This effect is called the Lead Time spiral and it happens in real life all the time. What happened, in this story, is that at some point the owner of Widget Manufacturing said enough. "I declare that starting Monday the Lead Times will be sixteen weeks and I'm starting another shift. The results! Several late deliveries but more importantly, for our discussion, demand dried up. When the Lead Time was reduced, much of the increased demand disappeared. Sure some hedging still went on, but the vast amount of increased demand simply disappeared."

"In the 70's companies went out of business because of the effects of the Lead Time spiral. Companies borrowed to increase capacity due to the perceived increased demand. When capacity increased, Lead Time shortened and the demand disappeared. The demand mirage disappeared and the reality of the Lead Time spiral left insufficient demand to cover the capital expenditures. Again, in the 90's, demand in the DRAM market disappeared when capacity increased and Lead Times decreased. This cost the vendors the money lost to increase capacity to support an imaginary demand profile. Furthermore, when the demand went away, the supply exceeded demand leaving no support for the current price/profit structure. Prices and profits dropped."

"Controlling this spiral is the job of planning, using input/output control. They monitor Demand vs. Capacity to control increased demand. They have only two choices: Increase output (capacity), or constrain demand. Planning offsets potential problems by increasing capacity through implementation of overtime, temporary additions of people and/or equipment, through sub-contracting and renting of capital equipment, or through the addition of manufacturing shifts. In addition they free up capacity by using alternate processes that utilize under capacity resources, or subcontracting work outside, or reduction in lot sizes (true Cycle Time reductions), and as a last resort a change in the master production schedule."

Input / Output Control

Week #	Last	Current	1	2	3	4	5
Planned Customer orders	1000	1000	1000	1200	1200	1200	1300
Actual Customer orders	1200	1100	1000	1300	1400	1200	1300
Planned vs. Actual	200	100	0	100	200	0	0
Cumulative Delta Input	200	300	300	400	600	600	600
Planned Output	1000	1000	1000	1200	1200	1200	1300
Actual Output	1200	1000					
Planned vs. Actual Output	0	0					
Cumulative Delta Input	200	0					
Planned Backlog	3000	3000	3000	3000	3000	3000	3000
Actual Backlog	3000	3100					
Total Delta Planned less Actual	0	-100					

"The table above represents an input/output control chart for a business. It shows that customer orders continue to meet or exceed the plan. Further, it shows output matching demand last week but not for the current week, adding to the backlog. If this business based its quoted Lead Time on this chart, this vendor would increase Lead Time. That is the wrong thing to do because that action starts the Lead Time spiral. This vendor has only two choices:

Increase output, or constrain demand. This table will show backlog getting progressively worse if quoted Lead Time was increased."

"One approach is:"

- ✓ "Base Lead Time changes on the formula: Lead Time equals backlog divided by capacity. Result: Lead Time changes with each new order and each order completion; it is infinitely variable and the Lead Time spiral begins."
- ✓ "Limit demand by increasing Lead Times. Result: The Lead Time spiral. Increasing Lead Times does not result in buying the vendor breathing room to drive down backlog; it creates additional phantom demand (hedging). No planning system in the world can operate effectively when the parameters used constantly change."

"A better approach:"

- ✓ "Increasing capacity as detailed above. Result: The demand profile reflects the market place and quoted Lead Time continue to be credible."
- ✓ "Allocation of capacity (supply). This gives the buyer a known supply. It gives the vendor a more accurate picture of the demand. Both receive the benefits of credible quoted Lead Times."

"The vendor's process should be:" I put up the following slides and said.

Managing Inventory • 85

Analyze input/output		
When demand exceeds capacity determine if the demand is short term or long term	**Short Term**	**Long Term**
	Determine strategy (Overtime, subcontracting, etc.)	Determine competitive position
		No Competitor / **Competition**
		Determine allocation/pricing strategy / Determine strategy to increase capacity

"Increasing Lead Time hurts both buyer and vendor. In the long run it hurts the vendor more as shown on this table."

Vendor	Buyer
Transactional activities for open orders increase as Lead Time increases.	Transactional activities for open orders increase as Lead Time increases.
Difficult to determine real vs. hedging demands.	Scrambling to find alternate sources.
A potential quality problem as production expediting increases.	Difficult to keep planning system up to date regarding Lead Times.
Poor customer relations as deliveries are missed and Lead Times increase.	Poor customer and vendor relations.
Risk of increasing capital expenditures to support phantom (hedging) demands.	Production problems as priorities are changed to keep production busy.

"The conclusion is that Lead Times cannot be infinitely variable. Lead Time cannot be calculated based on capacity because:"

- "Variable Lead Times violate the purpose and criteria of Lead Times i.e., to direct action by being credible, accurate and timely."
- "Increasing Lead Times cause buyer to build hedge inventories."
- "Hedge inventories inflate demand."
- "Inflated demand leads to unwarranted capital expenditure decisions."

$$\text{Workload} = \frac{\text{Demand} + \text{Backlog}}{\text{Capacity}}$$

"However, each vendor uses the formula as the tool for input/output control. This tool tells the user when demand exceeds capacity. The vendor then implements corrective action based on market conditions."

"Now let me go back to Bill's point number 3, "Normal operations do not force buyers or vendors to violate Lead Times."

"Based on what we have just covered I argue that vendors who base Lead Time length on the capacity formula, must change their way of doing business. That is because the answer derived from formula changes every time the calculation runs. Now you and I know that we can't live in that kind of changing world. We respond by inflating the Lead Time length as a hedge. Because the length exceeds what the vendor "knows" can be met, when a buyer needs an improved length (an expedite) the vendor responds, most often, favorably. The normal way of doing business becomes, what I call, Lead Time with a wink. 'Here is my Lead Time, but if you really need me to respond quicker it's OK.' We design in Lead Time lengths that violate the purpose and criteria of Lead Time."

"So for this point I'll write 'True only as long as the length is One Day.' Experience shows us that all other lengths do change of one reason or another."

"To this point I have created the impression that vendors are the cause of long Lead Times. But buyers also do their fair share in driving Lead Time length."

Chapter 9

BUYER'S EFFECT

ON QUOTED LEAD TIME

"Now I will turn to those purchased commodities that are not make-to-stock items (The short quoted Lead Time length for nuts, bolts, screws, other common items normally are not affected by the buyers conduct that I talk about here.)."

"Vendors do not set their Lead Times in a vacuum. The quantity a buyer asks the vendor to quote, and the information the buyer is willing to share with the vendor, often forces the vendor to respond in a specific manner. Let me explain"

Quantity

"When a buyer asks a vendor for a Lead Time quote on a quantity of between 10 and 10,000,000 it will more than likely, force the vendor to protect themselves by quoting a long Lead Time."

"The buyer asked for a quantity between 10 and 10,000,000 because the answer gives the buyer price options and costs structure intelligence. The format of the answer tells the buyer where price breaks exists and therefore some indication of the vendors fixed costs. Another reason for the quantity spread is that the buyer wants protection against an uncertain demand forecast. The answer the vendor provides indicates Lead Times as well as price breaks. Since the vendor usually does not give Lead Time ranges that match up with the quantity/price ranges, the Lead Time provided must cover the vendor in the worst case, i.e. the 10,000,000 quantity. Alternatively, the vendor, not knowing the demand picture, and living the 'Under-promise, Over-deliver' concept, quotes a Lead Time length that sufficient to meet a worse case scenario. Long Lead Times once entered into the planning system drive all the bad things defined earlier (high transactional costs, and high inventories)."

"Buyers, and vendors traditionally think that Lead Time length and price/quantity breaks go together based on this logic path:"

1. "The larger the manufacturing lot size the greater the potential price break, and"
2. "Large manufacturing lot sizes consume capacity, and"
3. "As capacity is consumed manufacturing flexibility decreases"
4. "Therefore price breaks drive longer Lead Times."

"However, when Lead Time length varies with capacity utilization, Lead Time looses credibility, and the buyers planning system looses its value. Remember the purpose and criteria of Lead Time:" I pointed to the wall charts.

- ✓ "Lead Time directs when an action must take place to insure a desired result."
- ✓ "Lead Times must be credible, adhered to, and changed only in advance of need."

"*Conclusion*: Quantity/price break calculations drive inventory levels. Quantity/price break calculations must be a separate issue from determining quoted Lead Time length. Furthermore, when considering quantity buys, the buyer must deal with the total cost of purchasing not just the purchase price. The vendor must also consider the total cost of producing when proposing a quantity price break including inventory and transactional costs."

"Next we have *demand uncertainty,* which is always a fact of business life. Earlier I talked about the magnitude of change in a forecast being directly proportional to the length of the forecast period. The further you look out the greater the probability and magnitude of change. We should accept that fact. Vendors like forecasts that they can rely on. When the vendor quotes a long Lead Time, because of the buyer's quantity spread, the result is self-defeating. Because the Lead Time length is long the probability and magnitude of demand forecast change is high. So the vendor forces a forecast they cannot rely on."

"So what can a body to do? The answer lies in the purpose of the forecast. When a vendors thinks of the forecast as a solid commitment, that vendors creates a self-defeating prophecy. The forecast must be thought of as the buyers best guess. It is to be used by the vendors for capacity purposes only, not to beat the buyer over the head because it changes."

Shared Information

"Any vendor has the right and the need, to know as much about the future as any buyer. I'm not talking about commitments, or an offer to buy. I'm talking about sharing the best information available at a point in time with the caveat that it is information only. The price for failing to share is excessive transactional costs and excess inventory. The perceived risk is that the vendor will hold the buyer financially liable for the forecasted quantities. When a buyer does not share forecasts, rate of use, and inventory information, the vendor is forced to make plans based on limited knowledge. This in turn forces the vendor to protect against change by quoted long Lead Times."

"Last chapter I said that a strategy used by a vendor when demand exceeds supply is to allocate quantities and raise prices. Buyers, who fail to share the best information available on forecasted demand, position themselves to be on the wrong end of a supply/demand relationship. This is not a one-way street. Sharing forecast information means that the vendor owes the buyer the assurance that capacity exists, or will exist to support the forecast. The key in this communication is integrity on both sides. The buyer must be willing to share how production capacity is able to consume the forecasted rate when requested to do so by the vendor. This is not a challenge; it is an exchange of information that supports a request. When a buyer needs to protect against competitors receiving advance production rate information, a confidentiality agreement with the potential vendor is the proper tool."

Lead Time Types

"Buyers sometimes ask for Lead Times quotes based on the amount of raw material or finished goods inventory available at the vendor's location. That is, when a product is in continuous production, the vendor probably has ongoing orders for raw materials. The fact that inventory exists, reduces the product Cycle Time which results in a lower quoted Lead Time. As opposed to a product the buyer purchases infrequently, where the buyer expects longer Lead Times. This yields two potential Lead Time lengths:"

- ✓ "*Infrequently ordered items* where the buyer assumes that little or no raw materials inventory exists and that production planning occurs upon receipt of the buyer's order."
- ✓ "*Normal production* typified by continuous production with frequent demands. Continuous replenishment of supply chain inventories drives shorter Lead Times."

Managing Inventory • 91

"This slide identifies the Lead Time (synonyms), production characteristics, and supply chain characteristics."

Lead Time (synonyms)	Production characteristics	Supply Chain characteristics
Worse case, Cold Start, Start-up Lead Time	New production, prototype, low volume	Request for quotes, infrequent demand
Normal, Response Time, Replenishment Time, Repetitive Lead Time	Normal or settled-down production. Higher volumes on production equipment.	Purchase orders with forecasts and contracts in place throughout the supply chain

"The buyer in asking for or defining, different Lead Times based on different definitions of Cycle Time drivers, is already on track with the idea that product Cycle Time does not drive Lead Time. By acknowledging that supply chain inventory affects Lead Time length, the buyer is part way to One Day Lead Times. Missing is a greater understanding of Lead Time drivers and the inclusion in the planning system of inventory's affect on Lead Time length."

"All that you're talking about has been a fact of life for years. It's the vendors job to figure out how to deal with them, not the buyers," A voice intoned.

"What I'm suggesting" I answered, "is that there is a better way to do business. A way that modifies the planning system thus making all the games we play unnecessary. That method is to establish One Day Lead Times regardless of the quantity ordered. Think about it, would any of this discussion take place if the vendor quoted One Day Lead Times?"

"Right" replied Bill, "none of this would be necessary if the vendors quoted One Day Lead Times. As I said before, vendor's must run their business in a manner that allows them to do that. It sounds to me like your addressing the wrong group here. You should be talking to sales, not procurement."

"Bill," I responded, "what do you perceive your responsibilities to your company to be, relative to procurement?"

"Among other things, to insure we get the most we can for the money we pay. To minimize our exposure and risk while maximizing our options relative to supply chain issues." Bill replied.

"OK. What do you perceive the sales force you interface with perceives its responsibilities to their companies to be," I asked.

Bill thought for a minute and then answered, "To maximize volume and profit while minimizing risk to their companies. That's just my point," he continued, "The apparent conflict you are talking about has to be resolved. The salesperson must convince me that they are helping me meet my responsibilities while they meet theirs. Again, you should be talking with them, not my group."

"Bill, there are some, though not in this room, who define 'Win-Win' as 'I win twice' I said. " I'm suggesting that the apparent conflict can, and should be, resolved through complete interchanges of information relative to procurement issues. Issues like long-term forecasts, rates of consumption, and, where necessary, methods that support those issues. That means the vendors do not receive the information as a method of holding the buyer hostage, and buyers do not give information as a way to manipulate the vendor. Information is a tool that helps both parties maximize their respective responsibilities. It is not a case of either/or, but a case of both. I have said that planning systems need Lead Times that are credible, adhered to, and timely. Likewise, business-to-business communications needs to be credible, adhered to, and timely."

❖ "Credible in that they reflect the best knowledge available at the time they are presented,"
❖ "Adhered to in that they reflect real world plans, not 'what if' scenarios, and"
❖ "Timely in that information is updated as change occurs."

"I am talking to you because it has to start somewhere. Why not with the buyer who is also a vendor. Remember when I went through the supply chain earlier I pointed out that each link is both buyer and vendor. So, by that logic Bill, when I talk to the vendor, I am also talking to the buyer. Beside that I have much to say to vendors after our break."

"Now, if there are no more comments, I'll get off my soap box and have a cup of coffee. See you later when I'll address the 'logic' used by some vendors to justify long Lead Times."

❖

❖

❖

Chapter 10

LEAD TIME DRIVERS

Refreshed, I start again.

"This portion of my presentation is mostly lecture. I thought of a more interactive format but backed off out of fear. I'm going to address what really drives Lead Time lengths. If I were to ask for your input, based on your experiences to date, I would force you into giving answers that I will then challenge. Why, because one of my premises is that most of us do not truly understand what really drives of Lead Time length. The proof. If we did understand, we would be living in a world of One Day Lead Times today. So, I lead you into giving answers that I then challenge. You in turn get upset that I led you down a wrong path. All that I present has a chance of getting lost in the emotion of the moment. So be patient while I lecture, we will have plenty of time for discussion later."

"Buyers may influence Lead Time length, but the vendor determines what length to quote. Many vendors explain that their Cycle Time is the driver of Lead Time length, but I will not accept that as the driver because, as I have shown, that logic results in variable Lead Times. Capacity constraints, change priorities, buyer changes, etc. end up driving variable Lead Times. To compensate for this variability some vendors add a time hedge onto product Cycle Time to cover for the unforeseen only to discover that that does not solve the problem. In the end, all vendors quoted Lead Times lengths are based on their perceived self-interest. Their logic goes like this:" I set up a slide as I continued to lecture.

Justification (logic) for Lead Time Length

- ❖ **Scarcity Logic**
- ❖ **Under promise, over deliver logic**
- ❖ **Security Logic**
- ❖ **Secure pay Logic**

- ❖ "Scarcity Logic"
  - ➢ "The laws of supply and demand govern the market place."
  - ➢ "When supply is controlled (perceived scarcity) a vendors market exists (a corollary is that the greater the scarcity the better for the vendor)."
  - ➢ "Long Lead Times create the perception of scarcity that is used to drive up prices/profits."
  - ➢ "Therefore, it is in the vendor's self-interest to have long Lead Times."

- ❖ "Under promise, over deliver logic"
  - ➢ "Murphy's law is alive and well. Something will go wrong in production."
  - ➢ "When I know I can better the quoted Lead Time, I know I will never be late. Vendors protect themselves from the unforeseen with long Lead Times."
  - ➢ "Long Lead Times allow the vendor to appear more flexible because they can, and do, react inside quoted Lead Times."

❖ "Security Logic"
  ➢ "Long Lead Times mean more firm (committed) orders on the books."
  ➢ "The greater the quantity of firm orders the longer I will continue to produce."
  ➢ "The longer into the future I produce the more I am sure of continuing in business."

❖ "Secure pay Logic"
  ➢ "Sales people who are paid on bookings, rather than shipments, maximize their pay check with long Lead Times because the quantity on order is greater than when Lead Times are short."

"Traditionally, from the vendor perspective, these logic paths take the form of the business practices adopted by the vendor. Those business practices are:" I set up another slide.

Business Practices

♦ **Competitive Advantage,**
♦ **Manufacturing Strategy, and**
♦ **The position of the product in its Life Cycle.**

"As long as we are dealing with traditional supply chain management, these three make up the Lead Time length determining factors we have to deal with. They disappear when the supply chain adopts One Day Lead Times, but until then, we have to deal with the world as it is. Knowing these facts is not enough. They must be quantified in order to perform valid comparisons. I have created a matrix that assigns values to the factors. Conversion of business practices into a value matrix allows the quantification of, and shows the interaction of, these practices. I subdivide each practice into its contributing factors. Assigning a rating from 1 to 10 to each factor yields a score for the vendor, or purchase item. The sum of the values predicts, or validates, the Lead Time logic used to quote by the vendor (the lower the score the shorter the quoted Lead Time). That is, the vendor makes Lead Time length decisions based on his or her view of the laws of supply and demand."

"Using my matrix quantifies the logic used by the vendor and replicates the vendor's logic. Low scores on one factor when offset set by high scores on other factors, demonstrate the interaction of the factors the vendor uses to establish Lead Time length. Vendors do not posses this matrix, nor do they have formal procedures that follow the logic I define here. However, they do through informal processes, set Lead Time lengths based on the factors contained in the matrix. After I define the factors, and their rationale, I address how to use that information in negotiating Lead Time length."

"NOTE: This is a guide based on the logic shown, vendors exist who understand the relationship between quoted Lead Time length and their own costs and therefore set Lead Time lower than this matrix indicates, those vendors already quote you One Day Lead Times."

As I defined each business practice, I hung up a sign with its definition.

1. *Competitive Advantage:*

"A buyer determines the competitive advantage based on eight criteria, Price, Quality, Deliverability, Flexibility, Product Design, Service, Image, and Technology. The buyer sets the relative weight of these factors based on their needs. Each buyer trades off the criteria to meet their needs. True, the vendor attempts to influence the buyer's perception through advertising and sales techniques, but the buyer makes the determination. And true the buyers seek vendors who are leaders in all criteria. But in the real world, reality and perception are not a perfect match. All scoring in the competitive advantage section is relative. It quantifies how the vendor being scored ranks on a scale of 1 to 10 relative to their competition."

   a) *Price*: "The amount paid by the buyer for an item. The score is based on these definitions:"
   - "Below competition (limited products) starts the scoring at 1."
   - "Equal to competition (or many products and lower than competitors price), continues through 5."
   - "Higher than competition (or sole source) has a top score of 10."

"Pricing principles are beyond the scope of this course except to state that price is based on the balance of the perceived competitive advantage and management philosophy. The lowest score option (a one) goes to those vendors whose prices are below competition, and who have a limited number of products. In order to minimize costs to support low pricing, the vendor passes the inventory onto the buyer. These vendors pass the high inventory to the buyer using minimum buy quantities, which they disguise as quantity/price brakes. They quote low Lead Times due to their continuous production mode."

"A middle range vendor stays close to their competition on price or beats their competition on price and has a broad product range. The later group manufactures large production quantities to keep costs low. The large runs limit their capacity, which reveals itself in their quoted Lead Time length."

"The highest score (a ten) goes to those who use supply and demand logic to their 'advantage.' High price and long quoted Lead Times justify each other in the practices of these vendors."

"*Examples:* The *Everything for $1* store competes on price. Everything is defined as everything they stock, not everything you want. The Lead Time varies from zero to infinity, in stock or not available. Items I purchased from distributors had the same distribution of Lead Time lengths."

"The price for a Harley-Davidson motorcycle is competitive when one considers that only Harley makes Harleys. If you want one, the price is, to you, very competitive but you are sole sourced. Harley defines the Lead Time."

"As a buyer I purchased items that were manufactured exclusively for my company, they had long Lead Times since the vendor controlled the market. Once selected that vendor thought that long Lead Times added to the perception of value to his product."

> b) "*Quality* is conformance to requirements, or fitness for use (the absence of defects). Vendors who use Six Sigma or SPC quality control techniques drive lower Cycle Times as a result. Vendors who do not build quality into their manufacturing process drive longer Cycle Times because of the amount of time required for rework, repair, and replacement of any defects found during inspection operations. Lower Lead Times are a reflection of lower Cycle Time when vendors believe the times are interdependent. *NOTE:* Remember that Lead Time length is a combination of these factors so a vendor whose quality control process drives a low Lead Time may have that factor outweighed by the sum of other business practices. The scoring range is:"

- "Six Sigma or SPC Quality Control — score as low as 1, no higher than 4."
- "Then progress through quality control processes equal to competition (or sole source) — score 5 – 7."
- "All the way to quality monitored through inspection — score at 8 through 10."

c) *"Deliverability* is the ability of a vendor to consistently meet agreed to delivery commitments. In my sample supply chain (Chapter 5) the final assembler put a hedge factor on Lead Time to protect against the unforeseen, thereby insuring a competitive advantage in deliverability. Most, if not all, service providers (dry cleaners, car service centers, etc.) quote Lead Times that insure deliverability accuracy. The scoring range for this factor is:"
- "Always late or early earns a low — score of 1."
- "Equal to competition (or sole source) — score goes on through 5."
- "Topping out at 100% on time — score of 10."

d) *"Flexibility* is the elapsed time taken by a vendor to satisfy any buyer request. The vendor defines how flexibility is accomplished. The flexible vendor provides the buyer with broad product line and the ability to add, delete and change quantities and required dates on short notice. The flexible vendor implements design changes quickly. Retailers, in general, allow high flexibility where custom vendors (tailors) do not."
- "Any change up to ship date allowed — score at 1 to 4."
- "Some changes allowed — score 5 to 7."
- "Few or no changes allowed — score 8 to 10."

e) *"Product Design* is the sum of product features and capabilities that differentiate the product from its competition. This includes options, features, and/or ascetics and the potential buyer defines these as a determining factor in product selection. Automobile companies, and many consumer electronic manufacturers, use product design to gain competitive advantage. Some vendors believe that design justifies a long quoted Lead Time. Score on this factor is based on the range of:"
- "Less features than the competition — scores start at 1."
- "Equal to competition — scores continues 5 through 7."
- "Finishing with more features than the competition — scoring 8 to 10."

f) *"Service* is support for a product, provided by a vendor, after the buyer receives the product. Whether the buyer owns, leases, or rents the product, service is measured by the amount of down time, and/or inconvenience, experienced when a problem occurs. Again, car dealerships attempt to gain a competitive advantage through the service level they provide. Examples of companies that promote service as a competitive advantage include:"
- "Mr. Goodwrench advertises its competitive advantage as service."
- "Caterpillar Corp. will provide a service part within twenty-four (24) hours or the part will be free."

"This provides Caterpillar with a competitive advantage in the service area when competitors do not match this promise. That does not mean either company quotes long Lead Times. These are examples to show how a traditional thought processes might justify long Lead Times when they use a competitive advantage in service as a consideration in setting Lead Time length. The scoring range for service is based on the following criteria:"

- "Better than competition starts at a 1."
- "Equal to competition score progresses through 7."
- "Below competition score tops at 10."

g) "*Image* is the value of a vendor, perceived by the buyer, based on the vendor's reputation for quality, service, price, innovation, and/or product design. Brand names like Eastman Kodak, Coke-a-Cola, and Disney all carry favorable images used by them as a competitive advantage. This factor affects quoted Lead Time using a scoring that:"
- "Starts below competition at 1."
- "Continues with Equal to competition around 5."
- "Ending with better than competition at 10."

h) "*Technology* is the designed in capabilities of a product that differentiate that product from its potential competitors. For example: the first company to introduce audio CD's had a technology advantage over those who supplied audiotape. Far Eastern electronic industry companies have been leaders in technology and use that factor as a competitive advantage. Its affect on Lead Time length is scored:"
- "Multiple sources a 1."
- "Limited competition a 5."
- "Sole source scores a 10."

"*Observation:* I have had clients that argued that to be competitive in today's marketplace each vendor must be competitive in all respects. That is to say, that no one can afford to be at a competitive disadvantage in any of the eight criteria defined above. However, each vendor, based on their analysis of their target markets, defines their competitive strategy. That strategy defines where they seek a competitive advantage, where they may simply be competitive, and where, if anywhere, they need not be aggressive to compete. Before I get beat up by those who cannot imagine a criteria where they need not compete let me remind you of those producers who have created, or benefited from, a competitive advantage so great they have buyers willing wait two years and pay a premium price for their product. Many luxury items fall into this category. In business, I have seen "bells and whistles" designed into products that put the buyer at a competitive disadvantage. Vendors naturally like to have a competitive advantage. That is how they grow their business. I experienced this when buying custom integrated circuits. As the buyer, I was at a competitive disadvantage because the custom part was available from one or a limited number of vendors. The lack of competition contributed to the vendor's price, and more often than not, to their Lead Time strategy."

"The success or failure of a business rests on decisions made relative to competitive advantage and the practices that grow out of those decisions. It is the responsibility of each buyer and vendor to understand their, and their counterparts, competitive position. Understanding means that each knows how their opposite number perceives them in each criterion and the effect of that perception on all other criteria. In negotiations, we refer to this as doing your homework. But Competitive Advantage is only a part of the homework"

I switched slides.

Business Practices

- **Competitive Advantage**
  An edge; e.g., a process, patent, management philosophy, or a distribution system, etc., that a vendor has that enables the vendor to control a larger market share or profit margin than the vendor would have without the competitive advantage
  (APICS Dictionary, 7th Edition).

- **Manufacturing Strategy**
  A collective pattern of decisions that act upon the formulation and deployment of manufacturing resources
  (APICS Dictionary, 7th Edition).

- The position of the product in its Life Cycle

2. Manufacturing Strategy

"We need to understand our and our vendors, manufacturing strategy because it directly affects their quoted Lead Time length. When put into place manufacturing strategies take one of the following forms:"

   a) *"Make-to-Stock* The vendor uses finished goods inventory to fill buyer needs. This strategy results in the highest inventory for the vendor and the shortest Lead Time for the buyer. The vendor performs production and raw material planning in anticipation of buyer orders. Manufacturing performed before and independent of actual buyer orders does not support volume price breaks. Manufacturers produce commercial items such as nuts, bolts, resistors, and most retail items in a make-to-stock environment. Because of the availability of inventory, the score assigned is one (1)."

b) *"Assemble-to-Order*: The product is finished or assembled after receipt of a buyer's order (NOTE: the APICS dictionary defines assemble-to-order as a subset of make-to-order. I treat them as different because the inventory needed to support Assemble-to-Order costs more than the inventory needed in a Make-to-Order environment). Planning and stocking of components, sub-assemblies, packaging, etc. takes place in anticipation of a buyer's order. Inventory quantities at the vendors (raw materials and sub-assemblies only, no finished goods) are relatively high to support shorter Lead Times. Assemble-to-Order manufacturers typically quote Lead Time lengths longer than in a Make-to-Stock environment, but much shorter than Make-to-Order. The Assemble-to-Order environment earns a score of five (5)."

c) *"Make-to-Order*: Buyer orders generate all action in support of these products. The supply chain is empty. The procurement of necessary materials and components starts in response to the buyer's order. The result, no inventory at the manufacturers and long quoted Lead Times lengths. A buyer should be able to correlate, in the vendors planning system, purchase orders for raw materials that match in quantity his/her order for the finished product. Examples of products produced in a make-to-order environment include capital equipment, and some make to buyer unique specification products. Because the supply chain is empty, Make-to-stock strategies score a ten (10)."

d) *"Engineer-to-order*: Products whose buyer specifications require unique engineering design or significant customization. Each buyer order results in a unique set of part numbers, bills of material, and routings (APICS Dictionary, 7th Edition). This strategy results in the longest quoted Lead Time but happens only once per product life, so the Lead Time does not drive inventory levels."

e) *"Combinations (Demand Flow Technology, Kan-Bans, etc):* In an effort to minimize inventories and maximize responsiveness, a small quantity of finished goods inventory supports buyer needs while final assembly is Assemble-to-Order. When the entire supply chain applies this environment low inventory and quick responsiveness earn a score of one (1)."

"Competitive Advantage and Manufacturing Strategy are two of three components that determine Lead Time strategy. The last factor is the position of a product in its life cycle."

Business Practices

- **Competitive Advantage**
  An edge; e.g., a process, patent, management philosophy, or a distribution system, etc., that a vendor has that enables the vendor to control a larger market share or profit margin than the vendor would have without the competitive advantage (APICS Dictionary, 7th Edition).

- **Manufacturing Strategy**
  A collective pattern of decisions that act upon the formulation and deployment of manufacturing resources (APICS Dictionary, 7th Edition).

- **The position of the product in its Life Cycle**
  The stages of product life cycle are introduction, growth, maturity, and decline.

3. Product Life Cycle

"The characteristics that define each are:"

I added another slide

Stage	Volume	Design Stability	Manufacturing Strategy	Normal Quoted Lead Time length*	Score
Introduction	Low	Many changes	Engineer-to-Order	Longest	10
Growth	Low to medium	Less change	Make-to-Order	Long	5
Maturity	High	Stable	Make-to-Stock or Assemble-to-Order	Shortest	1
Decline	Low	Stable	Make-to-Order	Long	10

*Normal Quoted Lead Time given equal competitive advantage and manufacturing strategy.

"Some interchangeability in this matrix exists where a vendor risks a manufacturing strategy of Make-to-Stock during the growth stage in order to gain market share at the expense of scrapping old designs. Stocking may also be an option during decline to reduce costs through larger manufacturing lots. With that caveat, remember the above acts as a guide to buyers and vendors, not and exact formulation."

"The setting of, and negotiation around, quoted Lead Times is, for the most part, a function of the business practices of the vendor. Where does the vendor see their Competitive Advantage? What is their Manufacturing Strategy? Where is the product in its Life Cycle? These factors drive Lead

Time length. The matrix on the next page allows you to rate each vendor/products' business practices on a scale of 1 to 10 for each factor. The buyer, the vendor, or both assign a score and the resultant total score provides a guide to the probable Lead Time for the product being rated."

"When negotiating Lead Times with vendors who resist quoting One Day Lead Times use this matrix as a guide to focus your discussion into areas of improvement. For instance: a vendor whose quality level is driven by a Six Sigma program will, by definition, drive lower Cycle Times than one who is not. All else being equal, that same vendor should demonstrate lower quoted Lead Times. If not, the focus of negotiations avoids the subject of quality, and concentrates on the issues that do drive the quoted Lead Time length."

"Be aware that some high scoring products and/or vendors may see no advantage to reducing their Lead Times because they rely on old paradigms. They believe long Lead Times support job security and price. They either change or risk the consequences when buyers apply the techniques shown in this book."

"*Transportation Cycle Time and Lead Time:* I would be remiss if I did not mention transportation Cycle Time somewhere in this discussion. We outsource some components, and/or sub-assemblies, in order to take advantage of lower labor rates. One price we pay for each item outsourced is increased quoted Lead Times to our buyers caused by transportation Cycle Time. Since limited options exist to influence transportation Cycle Time some amount of costs (transactional, etc.) become 'fixed.' Vendors insist that transportation Cycle Times drive some portion of their quoted Lead Time. Since you (the buyer) are responsible for the decision to outsource, you are responsible for insuring that your buyers (and you) do not suffer from your decision. Said another way, the buyer must be aware of supply chain length. When that length negatively affects the Lead Time quoted by the vendor, the buyer must hold the vendor responsible for the risks associated with long supply chains. The buyer need not accept longer than One Day quoted Lead Times caused by the vendors supply chain length. Chapter 16 deals with how to shelter the buyer from the effects of transportation Cycle Time."

"Selling Practices affect on Lead Time length: The setting of, and negotiation around, quoted Lead Times is, for the most part, a function of the business practices of the vendor. I say 'for the most part', because there is one additional factor that sometimes affects Lead Time length. That is the salesperson. The logic is much the same as supply demand logic. Here the salesperson increases bookings (open orders) by encouraging long Lead Times. The reason may have to do with the way in which the salesperson is compensated (pay or bonuses tied to bookings rather than deliveries), or the belief that a booked sale is hard to cancel. Just as buyers affect Lead Times based on their practices, salespeople just as easily influence Lead Time length based on their practices. The lesson: sales organization must know the buying practices of their buyers. Buyers must know the selling practices of their vendors."

"OK, end of lecture, lets talk. What is your reaction to what I've just said?"

Mary started, "Let me make sure I understand what you've said then ask the question." I nodded.

"Point one, Cycle Time does not drive Lead Time, right?"

"Not quite" I replied. "For many Cycle Time does drive Lead Time but what I'm saying is that it should not because the result is variable Lead Times. As I showed earlier, variable Lead Times neuter our planning systems and add costs to the buyer and to the vendor. I'll go one step further. Cycle Time *cannot* drive Lead Times in a business environment that utilizes a formal planning system because the resultant variable Lead Times neuter that planning systems and add costs to the buyer and to the vendor."

"Yes," Mary continued, "but then you say that business practices drive Lead Time. You can't have it both ways, which is correct?"

Smiling I replied "Both. This was driven home for me when I visited a vendor to negotiate Lead Time lengths. I discussed the factors we have covered and our discussion took over two hours. My goal had been to show what happens when we allow Cycle Time to drive lead Time. As usual, I thought I was brilliant, and persuasive. At the end the vendor looked at me and said 'Dave you are right, but I see no competitive reason to change.' That's when I realized that both conditions are true. That vendor's logic was to justify Lead Time length based on Cycle Time and then to use the Lead Time length to support maximized profits. In others words, the additional costs were offset by the high price that the long Lead Time 'supported'."

"I'm not sure I get your message" Mary said.

"Understandable" I said. "Lets look at that vendor using my Matrix." I wrote on the chart paper:

Lead Time Matrix

- Price was a 10, I was sole sourced, the part was an ASIC (application specific integrated circuit)
- Quality was a 5
- Deliverability was a 5
- Flexibility was a 5, because I could make changes within a defined time frame
- Product Design was a 10, due to the fact the part was designed in by my engineering group.
- Service, Image were 5's
- Technology was a 10
- Manufacturing Strategy was a 10 due to the design for me only
- And Position of product in its life Cycle was a 5.

"Total 70 points. The vendor owned me. I talked of future business and any thing else I could think of to try to compensate for my problems on this part, but on this item, I was in a very weak competitive position. With the matrix, I conducted internal negotiations to show my vendor had me at a competitive disadvantage. I met with the design and engineering groups to explain how this vendor cost us time, money and flexibility. My goal was to send a message back to the vendor, through engineering, as the definition of a competitive reason to reduce quoted Lead Time."

"That is why I say both Cycle Time and business practices. Because when vendors are educated on the effects of Lead Time, and buyers are educated on the drivers of Lead Time, the knowledge paves the way to One Day Lead Times."

"Have I answered your question Mary?"

"Let me say it back to make sure I understand you" Mary said. "Basing Lead Time on Cycle Time is no good because capacity constraints end up forcing the Lead Time to change as capacity fills and backlogs increase. And changeable Lead Times frustrate the planning system by forcing the buyer to protect themselves sometimes with hedge inventories. Right?"

"That's it," I replied

"Next, vendors base Lead Time length on their perception of their competitive position. Right?"

"Competitive position, manufacturing strategy, and the position of the product in its life cycle, " I responded.

"And you don't think that's a good idea either," she asked?

"I think there is a better way," I said. "The details I have to demonstrate to you, but that is basically what I'm saying."

"Well then," Mary said, "Show us the better way."

"OK, if there are no further questions? I'll continue," I promised.

"The goal is to understand, and then counter, the negative effects of those practices that increase Lead Time length. When a link in the supply chain will not reduce Lead Times the buyer has the option of compensating for that vendors long Lead Time."

"Before addressing compensating techniques, we need one more piece of data i.e. the affect of inventory on Lead Time length."

"Remember,
Cycle Time length is the result of a mathematical calculation (addition of Cycle Time elements),
Lead Time length is the result of a business decision."

Lead Time Matrix

	Factor	Criteria	Rating	Score
Competitive Advantages	Price	Below competition (limited products)	1	
		Equal to competition (or many products and lower than competitors price)	5	
		Higher than competition (or sole source)	10	
	Quality	Six Sigma or SPC Quality Control	1	
		Equal to competition (or sole source)	5	
		Quality through inspection	10	
	Deliverability	Always late or early	1	
		Equal to competition (or sole source)	5	
		100% on time	10	
	Flexibility (changes to open orders)	Any change up to ship date allowed	1	
		Some changes allowed	5	
		No changes allowed	10	
	Product Design (features and options)	Less features than the competition	1	
		Equal to competition	5	
		More features than the competition	10	
	Service (after sales)	Better than competition	1	
		Equal to competition	5	
		Below competition	10	
	Image (Vendor's rank in the marketplace)	Below competition	1	
		Equal to competition	5	
		Better than competition	10	
	Technology	Multiple sources	1	
		Limited competition	5	
		Sole source	10	
Manufacturing Strategy		Make-to-Stock	1	
		Assemble-to-Order	5	
		Make-to-Order	10	
Position of product in its Life Cycle		Mature product (high volume)	1	
		Growth (or low volume)	5	
		Introduction or Decline	10	
		Total		

Score
- 10 - 15   Expect very short Lead Times (< one week)
- 16 - 30   Moderate Lead Times (one to four weeks)
- 31 - 60   Long Lead Times (four to 15 weeks)
- Above 61   Very long Lead Times (over 15 weeks)

❖

❖

❖

Chapter 11

THE EFFECTS OF INVENTORY ON LEAD TIME

"We saw in our sample supply chain (Chapter 5) that available inventory allows a vendor to quote a Lead Time that is lower than Cycle Time. I also pointed out that the trick is to systemically define and control the quantity of inventory. Let's start with the effect of inventory on Lead Time. Looking at the product Cycle Time we see two places where an influx of inventory would allow the vendor to quote short Lead Times. The first is finished goods inventory."

Finished goods inventory neutralizes all Lead & Cycle Times to this point. ⎯⎯⎯

Sub Assembly Vendor			
Order Core Material	Raw Material Lead Time	Manufacturing Cycle Tme	Ship
2 days	48 days	5 days	1 day
Total Cycle Time is the sum of all activities (2 + 48 + 5 + 1) 56 Days			
Lead Time is set by the vendor The Sub Assembler quotes 6 Days Lead Time			

1. "*Finished goods* inventory allows the vendor to filter the buyer from the effects of manufacturing

Cycle Time and raw material Lead Time (Product Cycle Time). The buyer sees only a One Day Lead Time. This is in fact the way most retailers run their businesses. It is the way most manufacturers run that part of their business that deals directly with consumers when they utilize distribution centers (finished goods inventory storage). The amount of finished goods inventory required drives the cost of that inventory."

The second option is raw material and sub-assembly inventory.

Raw Material ———		Finished Goods Inventory ———	
Sub Assembly Vendor			
Order Core Material	Raw Material Lead Time	Manufacturing Cycle Tme	Ship
2 days	48 days	5 days	1 day
Total Cycle Time is the sum of all activities (2 + 48 + 5 + 1) 56 Days			
Lead Time is set by the vendor The Sub Assembler quotes 6 Days Lead Time			

2. "Since finished goods are more expensive (accumulated costs) than raw materials (no labor costs added) shifting inventory to raw materials is more cost effective inventory. *Raw materials* inventory negates the effect of raw material Lead Time on the product Cycle Time. That means that the amount of finished goods inventory necessary to meet changing buyer demands decreases. A relatively small

amount of finished goods meets short term demand changes backed up by raw material inventory used to meet longer term buyer demand changes."

"Wow stop" cried Bill. "You just spent a fair amount of time showing us how Cycle Time does not drive Lead Time. Now you say having more inventory allows us to quote short Lead Time because it compensates for Cycle Time. What's wrong with this picture?"

"There are only two things that need amendment in you question," I replied. "I did not say Cycle Time *does not drive* Lead Time, I said Cycle Time *cannot drive* Lead Time because the result will be variable Lead Times that neuter planning systems. Second I did not say *more inventory*, I said *inventory*. In fact, what I will show is that, relative to today, less systemically controlled inventory compensates for Cycle Time and drives One Day Lead Times. The distinctions are the keys to improvement. We are looking at the way we think about inventory and time for opportunities. I'm suggesting that my One Day Lead Times process presents a vastly superior way of managing inventory and time. Ok?"

"OK" said Bill.

"As quoted Lead Time length decreases forecast accuracy increases, i.e. the number of change requests to open orders decreases. The result is a double pay back:"

- "Finished goods inventory reduced due to shorter Cycle Time."
- "Finished goods inventory reduced due to greater forecast accuracy."

"The supply chain links I showed above demonstrate the logic and support the fact that inventories allows any link in a supply chain to quote a lower Lead Time. Neither the logic nor the graphic suggests that the current inventory quantities have to be increased to meet this goal. In fact they suggest the opposite."

"This is where I address Bill's point number 5, "The vendors ability to react must not be the result of inventory for which the buyer is liable."

"Empirically defining the amount of inventory and including that calculation in the planning system yields systemic control of inventory, i.e. inventory management. My experience showed that reducing quoted Lead Times in a circuit board assembly area, annual sales of $50,000,000, from 150 days to One Day netted a supply chain inventory reduction. The circuit board assembly area increased finished goods inventory levels by $3,000,000. The buyers reduced their inventories by $10,000,000. One Day Lead Times delivered a $7,000,000 reduction in supply chain inventory and a reduction in our buyer's product Cycle Time of 149 days."

Planning Systems Drive Inventory Quantities

"There are two facts about inventory:"

1. "All links in a supply chain that are not Make-to-Order or Engineer-to-Order plan to carry inventory as part of their production plan."
2. "Inventories allow any link in a supply chain to improve responsiveness to changing buyer needs."

"I demonstrated fact number two where I showed the vendor quoting lower Lead Times because they kept finished goods inventory. Fact number one exists because economies of scale exist in purchasing departments (exacerbated by the marketing techniques of vendors). In other words, setting aside JIT programs for a second, buyers do not buy quantities that meet immediate needs but rather they buy to a stocking strategy."

"Up to this point I have given the impression that all inventory is bad, that is not the case. Excess inventory is bad. How much inventory is excessive? For raw materials, the answer lies in the purchasing plan or stocking strategy of the buyer. Non-JIT industrial and retail buying planning systems determine buy quantities based on a planning systems that calculates buy quantities based on some formulation that is time based. That formulation may be an A, B, C policy, a restocking plan, or a minimum order quantity, etc. The result is an inventory profile that looks like a saw tooth pattern over time:"

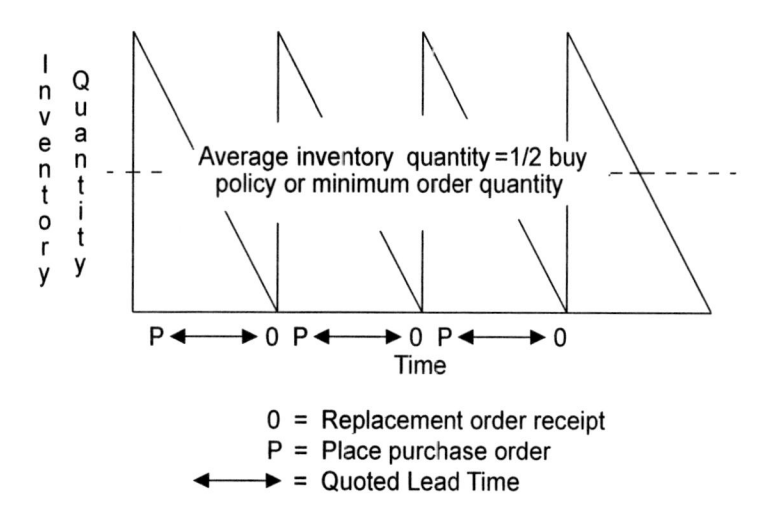

```
  I
  n   Q
  v   u
  e   a   |\      |\      |\      |\
  n   n   | \     | \     | \     | \
  t   t   |  \    |  \    |  \    |  \
  o   i   |   \   |   \   |   \   |   \
  r   t   Average inventory quantity = 1/2 buy
  y   y   policy or minimum order quantity
          |     \ |     \ |     \ |     \
          |      \|      \|      \|      \
          P◄──►0 P◄──►0 P◄──►0
                    Time
```

    0 = Replacement order receipt
    P = Place purchase order
    ◄──► = Quoted Lead Time

"Granted the actual inventory levels are not as symmetrical as this picture, but the representation does shows that we use inventory over time. The picture shows that, on average, your planned inventory quantity is ½ your purchasing plan or stocking strategy. Therefore, by definition, your excess inventory equals actual on-hand inventory less planned inventory or stocking strategy."

"The angled line represents the actual amount of inventory on hand. Moving backward in time from the zero point just in front of the (0) then looking up at the sloped line depicts how much inventory is planned to be available at that time. Looking up from the "P" point depicts the quantity of inventory on hand at the time you place a new order with a vendor. As you can see, the longer the quoted Lead Time (the distance between 0 and P) the greater the quantity of on-hand inventory at the time of order placement. Since we know that forecasts always change, this means the greater the Lead Time the greater the probability that the quantity of inventory at time of receipt will be incorrect. Or, the greater the quoted Lead Time the greater the amount of inventory that may not be used while waiting for the replacement order. Conversely, the longer the Lead Time, the greater the amount of time for potential stock outs. Since it is business facts that it is better to have inventory than to have stock outs, is it any wonder that inventories are normally higher than ½ buy policy (stocking strategy) or minimum order quantity."

"Now we know two things." I put up a slide.

---

1. **Planned inventory exceeds current needs i.e. we carry excess raw material inventory by design (buy policies define planned inventory).**
2. **Inventories (Safety Stock) carried by the vendor allow the vendor to quote short Lead Times.**

"However, these facts will do nothing to reduce quoted Lead Times unless the planning system supports the use of inventory as a guard against unforeseen changes in supply or demand. Planning systems must manage safety stock not simply track inventory."

"After a review of what we have covered so far, that is what I will address next." But first any questions about inventory?"

I looked around the room and saw no blank faces so I continued.

Chapter 12

SUMMARY

"OK folks, we have reached a major break point. I am going to click off what we have covered to this point. I will detail the conclusions that we have drawn from what we have learned. As I do so I will refer to the chapter where the topic was covered so that you can review the facts at your leisure. For now, as I click these off, interrupt me when, or if something is not clear. If you simply disagree, then I ask you to refer to the reading material again." I started to flip through slides and summarizing everything we had covered to this point.

"Chapter 1"

- "One of a planning systems functions is to use time to calulate the start or finish times of all activities that support a specific outcome given a desired start or finish time."
- "*Lead Time* is the amount of time, defined by the vendor, required to meet a request of demand."

"Chapter 2"

- "For the planning system to function properly and, and for our businesses to operate effectively, the Lead Times entered into the planning system must be credible, adhered to, and timely."

"Chapter 3"

- "*Cycle Time* is the sum of actual or allocated times necessary to complete an operation or process."
- "Cycle Time reduction *is the key* to improved quality, reduced costs, and inventory reduction."

"Chapter 4"

- "Lead Time and Cycle Time appear to us to be the same because we have experienced the ability to change both. We unconsciously mix them as part of our normal life."
- "As buyers we always know our vendors Lead Time, we do not always know their Cycle Time. As a planner we always know an operations Lead Time we do not always know the actual Cycle Time."

"Chapter 5"

- "Lead Time can be equal to, greater than, or less than Cycle Time."
- "In a multi level supply chain a product's Total Cycle Time is hidden because:"
  - "Each link in a supply chain can only see the Lead Time of the previous link."
  - "Vendor quoted Lead Time is an element in a link's product Cycle Time."
- "The vendor always defines Lead Time length (a buyer can negotiate but the vendor makes the business decision)."
- "A Lead Time reduction anywhere in the supply chain is a Cycle Time reduction at the next link."

- "Cycle Time length is always defined by the process."
- "Each link's product Cycle Time is the sum of its process Cycle Times and the longest Vendor quoted Lead Time."
- "Cycle Time is to Lead Time as Cost is to Price, they are related but one does not drive the other."

"Chapter 6"

- "Lead Time can be shorter, equal to, or longer than the product Cycle Time."
    - "Quoted Lead Time lengths set to equal Cycle Time lengths force the vendor to violate Lead Time criteria as capacity constraints and conflicting production priorities yield variable quoted Lead Times."
    - "Quoted Lead Times set greater than Cycle Times violate Lead Time criteria because they are not credible, adhered to, or timely as vendors can, and do, change quoted Lead Times to meet needs."
    - "Quoted Lead Times set lower than Cycle Time meet Lead Time criteria while allowing greater buyer service and lower transactional costs, but at the cost of inventory."

"Chapter 7"

- "Quantifying the cost of Lead Time."
  - "Costs increase (Each of these costs can be quantified and tracked)."
- "Increased transactional activities for the vendors in terms of production planning and sales, for the buyer in terms of purchasing activities."

"Potential change requests = (# of scheduled deliveries * # of system updates) * cost of activity"

- "Increased inventories. When planned raw material inventory levels are driven by buy policies, measured as inventory turns or in dollars, then:"

"Planned Inventory Dollars = ½ (buy policy or stocking strategy * Purchase price)"
"Or"
"Planning Inventory Turns = days per year / ½ days of supply per purchase"

"The cost of current Lead Times (in terms of excess inventory we carry) equals actual inventory – planned inventory."

- "Production planning disruptions are measured the same as transactional activities."
  - "Buyer service decreases for all parties affected when measured as the number of change requests not met."
  - "Buyer's and Vendor's effectiveness decreases (costs increase measured as the sum of the above)."

"Chapter 8"

- "Lead Time cannot be calculated based on capacity because:"
    - "Variable Lead Times violate the purpose and criteria of Lead Times i.e., to direct action by being credible, accurate and timely."
    - "Increasing Lead Times causes the buyer to build hedge inventories."
    - "Hedge inventories inflate demand."
    - "Inflated demand leads to unwarranted capital expenditure decisions."

"Use the formula as the tool for input/output control."

$$\text{Workload} = \frac{\text{Current Demand} + \text{Backlog}}{\text{Capacity}}$$

"Chapter 9"

- "Vendors do not set their Lead Times in a vacuum. The quantity a buyer asks the vendor to quote, and the information the buyer is willing to share with the vendor, often forces the vendor to respond in a specific manner."
- "Quoted Lead Time length determination is separate from quantity/price break calculation."

"Chapter 10"

- "In the end, vendors quote Lead Time lengths based on their perceived self-interest. Lead Time length is the result of a business decision."
- "Traditionally, from the vendor perspective, this logic takes the form of the business practices adopted by the vendor. Those business practices are:"
  - "Competitive Advantage,"
  - "Manufacturing Strategy, and"
  - "The position of the product in its Life Cycle."
- "Knowing these facts is not enough. They must be quantified in order to perform valid comparisons."
- "Conversion of business practices into a value matrix allows the quantification of, and shows the interaction of, these practices."

"Chapter 11"

- "Looking at the product Cycle Time, we see two places where an influx of inventory would allow the vendor to quote short Lead Times."
  - "*Finished goods* inventory allows the vendor to filter the buyer from the effect of manufacturing Cycle Time and raw material Lead Time."
  - "*Raw materials* availability (in stock as inventory) negates the effect of raw material Lead Time on the product Cycle Time."
- "All links in a supply chain that are not "Make-to-Order" or "Engineer-to-Order" *plan* to carry inventory as part of their production plan."

Managing Inventory • 131

"What does all this add up to?"

- ❖ "Vendors set Lead Time lengths based on their business practices, not based on Cycle Time. The results include excess costs, excess inventory, and erratic production schedules."
- ❖ "All organizations who deal with Lead Times greater than one day need resources to:"
  - ➤ "Attempt to change open orders when the existing promise date does not meet current needs."
  - ➤ "Shift production priorities when promised delivery dates are missed."
  - ➤ "Attempt to control the inventory that grows as buyers protect against uncertainty with hedge that sets unused because demands lessen during Lead Time."

- ❖ "One Day Lead Times reduce costs, and inventories. Sense business practices set Lead Time length, a new business practice defining Lead Time length as One Day is possible."
- ❖ "One Day Lead Time lengths can be achieved quickly through the use of safety stock, however most planning systems do not correctly allow safety stock to be used as it is intended to be used. Nor do they provide a tool to calculate the quantity of safety stock needed to support quoted One Day Lead Times."
- ❖ "A method is needed to correctly calculate the amount of safety stock required, and allow that safety stock to be used in support of One Day Lead Times. If that method protects the production schedule from erratic changes, that would be a bonus."

❖ "Cycle Time reduction programs are the key to maximizing cost and inventory reductions while improving quality, but they take time to implement. So when One Day Lead Times, that work quickly, meet all the needs outlined above and free up resources to work on Cycle Time reduction programs, everybody wins."

"Lastly, where do we stand with Bill's concerns?" I pointed to Bill Chart.

Concerns	Answers
1. The planning system requires repeatable data.	1. Agreed! When they are Credible, Adhered to and timely.
2. The planning system does not require frozen data.	2. True See 1 above
3. Normal operations do not force buyers or vendors to violate Lead Times.	3. True only as long as the length is One Day. Experience shows us that all other lengths do change of one reason or another.
4. Vendors must be able to meet customer's demands.	4.
5. That vendor's ability to react must not be the result of inventory for which the buyer is liable.	5.
6. The key to vendor responsiveness lies in their ability to reduce Cycle Times.	6. Yes until capacity restricts the ability to meet demand.
7. The effects of Lead Time length.	7. Costs increase as Lead Time length increases.

"I still have to answer concerns 4 and 5, and I will."

"It is time to move on. Time to take advantage of this knowledge. Time to take up the challenges. It is time we implement the One Day Lead Times Process. But first, it is time for lunch. See you in an hour."

Chapter 13

PLANNING SYSTEMS AND INVENTORY

"Again to avoid embarrassing anyone I'll ask a rhetorical question. How many of you will agree with this statement."

"Our planning systems fight us using safety stock as intended." I waited for this to sink in before continuing. They were not comfortable but took me at my word; after all, it was a rhetorical question.

"To explore this we need to agree on the definition and purpose of safety stock."

I wrote the definition of safety stock on the chart.

"Safety stock is the quantity of an item set aside to cover for changes in supply or demand inside Lead Time (APICS Dictionary 7th Edition).

"Safety Stock allows the vendor to offer schedule and quantity flexibility to the users of the product. Sometimes the increased flexibility is translated into reduced quoted Lead Times to buyers. If not, then at least the vendor reacts quickly to new or increased orders for product. Raw material safety stock allows a manufacturer to replace lost or damaged components without interruption to the manufacturing area. Safety stock allows a link in a supply chain to compensate for poor vendor delivery performance. In short, many of us have been trained to believe that safety stock, under the right conditions, saves our bacon. We 'know' that the cost of safety stock is outweighed by its saving power. The planning system treats safety stock as supply chain performance insurance."

"*What performance insurance does Safety Stock purport to provide?*" I listed the answers.

Safety stock protects against:

- **Interruption in supply.**
- **Unforecasted increases in demand.**
- **Interruption in supply at the same time as an unforecasted increase in demand.**

Safety stock does not protect against:

- **Engineering changes**
- **Unforecasted demand decreases**

"To address the first point, interruption in supply and increased demand, let's run an example. The table below contains elements found in all planning systems i.e. dates, demand quantities, open order supply quantities, projected inventory quantities, suggested supply quantities (the comment section is added for clarity). The item in this example has a Lead Time of 6 weeks (30 days), and a buy policy (stocking strategy) of 8 weeks (40 days). *Italics represent the date a message would appear for buyer action.*"

Managing Inventory • 135

Sample material planning report

Date	Demand	Supply	Inventory	Comment	Suggested Order Qty
11/2/96			396	On-Hand	
11/2/96	200		196	Safety Stock	
11/9/96	150		46	Planned Requirement	
11/14/96		1886	1932	Planned open order receipt	
11/16/96	196		1736	Planned Requirement	
11/23/96	225		1511	Planned Requirement	
11/30/96				*Message on buyer's report to place an order to meet the demand of 1/11/97.*	
11/30/96	360		1151	Planned Requirement	
12/7/96	300		851	Planned Requirement	
12/14/96	250		601	Planned Requirement	
12/21/96	196		405	Planned Requirement	
12/28/96	206		199	Planned Requirement	
1/4/97	199		0	Planned Requirement	
1/11/97	256		-256	Planned Requirement	1978
1/18/97	315		-571	Planned Requirement	
1/25/97	300		-871	Planned Requirement	

"This example shows, again, the system inventory level at the time the buyer is instructed to place a new order. My purpose is more. Look at inventory levels throughout the buy cycle, which is every 8 weeks. Does this planning system reflect actual on-hand inventories?"

"Specifically, on December 21, 1996 is the on-hand inventory 405 units?"

I waited for an answer. "Yes" volunteered Mary.

"No" added Pete.

"Why yes and no" I asked, "Mary you first."

"Because," Mary started, "one of the planning system's jobs is to tell the buyer and planner the quantity of an item available for use on a specific date. That is what is being shown on December 21, 405 units available for use."

"Thank you, Mary, your turn Pete" I said.

"Taking my clue from your introduction," Pete started, "On December, 21 there are 605 units in inventory, made up of 405 units available and 200 units reserved for safety stock. By the way," he continued, "I have no problem with that information. What I need to know is the amount available and, since I lost my crystal ball, I want those 200 available to cover me in case of a problem."

"Good, we are on the same page. Let's continue," I said.

"Your answers do not conflict even if I implied they do. What's important, what we need to discuss, are the implications of your answers, and the opportunity they present."

Planning systems do not report actual inventory quantities including safety stock.

"Planning systems tend to consume safety stock; that is how they protect it from being used. To the planning system, safety stock is the same as any other demand. If an unforecasted demand appeared on January 4, 1997, the planning system would show that the demand could not be met because of an inventory balance of zero. If a request from a buyer asked that the demand scheduled for January 11, 1997 be moved up a week, the planning system would say *NO* again because of zero inventory."

"The definition of safety stock is 'the quantity of an item set aside to cover for changes in supply or demand inside Lead Time'. There are 200 units of safety stock on-hand. Yet, the planning system consumed them making them unavailable for use. Doesn't this violate the definition of safety stock?"

"What do some of us do? A planner looks at the safety stock and sees it is available, so the planner overrides the system recommendation and commits all or part of the safety stock for use. The system has no way of knowing this unless the planner changes the system to reflect the quantity committed. Saving that, what does the planning system do? It asks the buyer to replace the used safety stock units on the date projected available inventory is negative. Let's look again."

I put up another slide and pointed as I talked. "Example: Today is 12/1/96, as the buyer, I look at the planning system buyers report and see a new demand for 100 units on 12/28/96 in addition to the 206 unit previously planned demand. (I'll also show an additional column of numbers [in bold] that reflect actual on-hand inventory. This column does not appear in planning systems.)"

Date	Demand	Supply	Inventory	Actual Inv.	Comment
12/1/96			1351	**1351**	On-Hand Inventory
12/1/96	200		1151	**1351**	Safety Stock
12/7/96	300		851	**1051**	Planned Requirement
12/14/96	250		601	**801**	Planned Requirement
12/21/96	196		405	**605**	Planned Requirement
12/28/96	306		99	**299**	Planned Requirement
1/4/97	199		-100	**100**	Planned Requirement Message on Buyers report
1/11/97		1978	1878	**2078**	Planned open order receipt

"The planning system generates a message telling the buyer to expedite the 1978 unit planned open order receipt due 1/11/97 to cover the negative inventory of 1/4/97. But there is no negative inventory!"

"The results of the safety stock in a planning system are:"

- ❖ "The buyer ignores expedite messages when reviewing the planning system messages because the safety stock quantities are sufficient to meet the short-term need."
- ❖ "Ignoring messages means that the buyer loses faith in the planning system. 'We spend a zillion dollars on systems that don't tell me what I need to know.'"

  "OR, the buyer attempts react to the planning system information by:"
  - ➢ "Decreasing the safety stock quantity in the planning system to reflect the commitment then."
  - ➢ "Placing an order for replacement of committed safety stock quantity."
  - ➢ "Records or memorizes what has been done so that"
  - ➢ "Upon receipt of the replacement quantity, the buyer increases the safety stock quantity back up to the original quantity, assuming no other changes have occurred."

    "Now assume the buyer reacted to the planning systems expedite message as it appeared."
    - ♦ "When the buyer calls the vendor to expedite the open order, that vendor believes that the buyer cannot forecast needs accurately even a few weeks into the future."
    - ♦ "To protect against short-term changes from the buyer, the vendor increases quoted Lead Time and starts another version of the Lead Time spiral."

      "NOTE: If Electronic Commerce exists, the expedite messages sent to vendors contains inaccurate information."

"Now, take any Bill of Materials, for any product and add safety stock to each item. Take the effects shown above and multiply them times the number of items on your bill times the frequency with which the planning system is updated. Is it any wonder that stock-outs occur while excess inventory and safety stock exists?"

"Safety stock, loaded into most planning systems, is unmanageable and will not insure against stock outs".

"But!... Each time the buyer/planner uses safety stock to react to a request inside Lead Time they become heroes in the view of their managers."

"Each time the buyer/planner reacts to a request inside Lead Time they loose credibility with that same requester because the planner/buyer reacted favorably to that same inside Lead Time change request (the requestor does not know what the real lead time is)."

"There is something fundamentally wrong with this picture".

"The statement 'Safety stock is the quantity of an item set aside to cover for changes in supply or demand inside of Lead Time' is an oxymoron when the planning system consumes the safety stock thus making it unavailable for its intended use. As I have demonstrated throughout this course, the last thing we want to do is respond inside Lead Time. By definition, Lead Times, in a planning system, must be credible, adhered to, and timely. Violating those criteria is a costly business error. Mary and Pete, you are both right in your desire to have safety stock available to meet needs. That does not mean, however, that you want safety stock available to violate the Lead Time you quote. See what I'm driving at here, there is a difference between meeting needs and violating quoted Lead Times, just as there is a difference between managing inventory and tracking inventory. That is why I push for One Day Lead Times. We want One Day Lead Times that never need to be beat. Said another way: buyers must be protected from the historic effects of changes in supply or demand. The definition of Safety Stock must be " Safety stock is the quantity of a item set aside to support One Day quoted Lead Times to the next link in the supply chain and/or changes is supply."

"How can we accomplish this? I go into detail later, but here is my recommendation. Modify the planning system so that the systems updates detailed above do not happen within an item's Lead Time as long as safety stock exists."

I looked at Mary and Pete; they were nodding but less than enthusiastic. Ok I said to myself, we'll verify when I get to the "how to do it" stage. I paused for a few seconds to allow anybody to challenge what I had just said. When no one raised a hand, I continued.

"Does your planning system fight the use of safety stock? Look at a materials planning report to check for the following:" I put up the list.

- ✓ Does your system consume safety stock as I showed earlier?
- ✓ Does your system send buy and/or expedite messages to the buyer, inside vendor quoted Lead Time, because it does not consider safety stock as available for use?

"If your answer to these questions is YES, then I say it again; 'our planning systems fight us using safety stock as intended.' We do not reduce quoted Lead Times to buyers when we have the inventory to support a reduction. And, we do not use safety stock to support short quoted Lead Times."

"Bottom line—Planning systems do not use traditional safety stock, in a manner that is consistent with the purpose of the planning system."

Vendor's perspective "As a vendor to a buyer that maintains safety stock, you are on the receiving end of the changes shown above. That means that as the buyer at-

Managing Inventory • 141

tempts to balance inventory based on planning system messages, you are asked to continuously change your open orders with that buyer. Your costs increase and your faith in the buyer goes down. Your natural tendency is to blame the buyer, however the fault lies with you, the vendor. Vendors must ask themselves this question: 'Would any of this happened if I were to quote the buyer One Day Lead Times?' I'll summarize." I put up a slide.

Traditional Safety Stock

Strong Points	Weak Points
Increases responsiveness	• Quoted Lead Time is not credible or accurate. • Lower Lead Times may not be repeatable. • Buyers may expect a level of flexibility not sustainable by the vendor. • Adversarial relations result from apparent arbitrary granting of expediting requests from buyers (buyers will push the envelope). • Increased difficulty in negotiating premiums for expediting.
Fits in with current planning system software logic	• Forces inventory levels higher than optimal. • Quantity is not empirically determined. How much safety stock is correct? • No process in place to calculate what Lead Time should be quoted to a buyer. • No process is in place to calculate which product(s) have safety stock. • Users lose faith in system-generated information.

"As buyers and vendors, we know that inventory (safety stock) allows any link in a supply chain to quote One Day Lead Times to the next link. However, our planning systems do not support the systemic use of safety stock for Lead Time reduction. The problem is not the safety stock, the problem is the quoted Lead Times supported by long Cycle Times and unresponsive planning systems. Our challenge is to eliminate those problems."

❖

❖

❖

Chapter 14

USE OF PLANNED EXCESS RAW MATERIAL INVENTORY TO REDUCE LEAD TIME (PRACTICAL LEAD TIME CALCULATION)

"APICS defines excess inventory as 'Any inventory in the system that exceeds the minimum amount necessary to achieve the desired throughput rate at the constraint.' The way that organizations do business creates excess inventories. Buyers create excess inventory when the quantity of product purchased for a single delivery (often referred to as the stocking strategy) exceeds the immediate need. I referred to these earlier as A, B, C buy policies, reorder point quantities or stocking quantities. The fact that the procurement process has fixed costs associated with it drives the purchased quantities. Economies of scale leads one to the conclusion that the greater the quantity procured for a single delivery, the lower the unit cost of the procurement process. We understand that economies of scale logic is an impediment to Cycle Time reduction process, but until we eliminate all waste in the procurement process we need to deal with the world as it is, i.e. economies of scale. The saw tooth represents inventory levels created by stocking strategies. All inventory quantities above immediate need are by definition excess inventory. We rationalize the quantity, but it's still excess inventory."

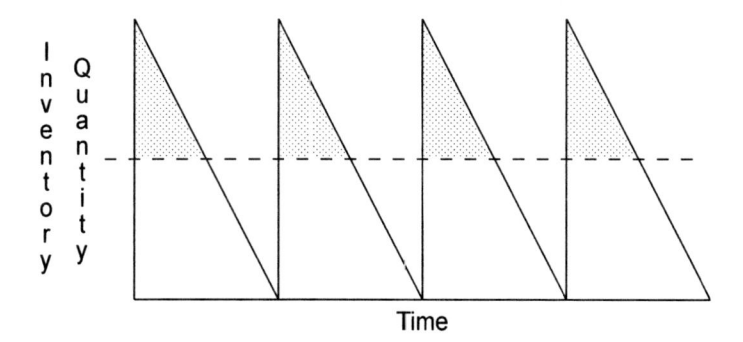

[Figure: Inventory/Quantity vs. Time sawtooth graph with dashed average line]

"The average quantity of excess inventory equals ½ the buy policy or minimum order quantity (the shaded area of the triangle). Why? Because we consume purchased inventory over time. Therefore, immediately after an order receipt most of the inventory is excess inventory. Over time, the quantity of excess inventory decreases. I generalize this fact with the statement: excess inventory equals ½ the buy quantity. I watched this effect in the production area for years. A customer would call to increase an order, or to move in a delivery. The degree of difficulty in meeting the request was relative to my quoted Lead Time for the product requested." I drew a triangle on the chart paper.

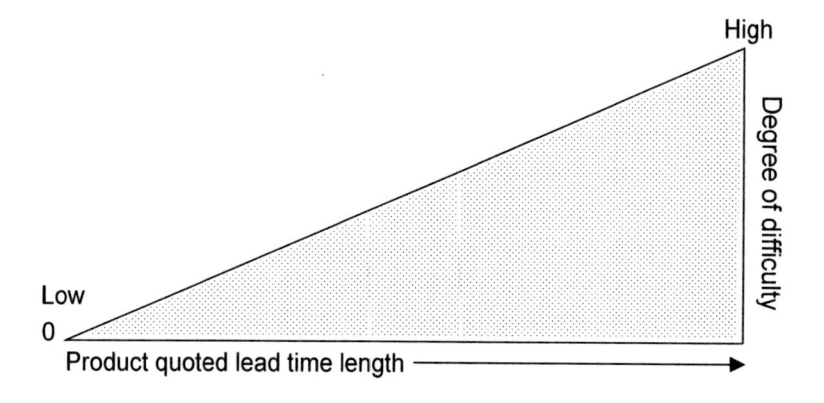

[Figure: Triangle graph showing Degree of difficulty (Low to High) vs. Product quoted lead time length]

"A small percentage change, relative to product quoted Lead Time would cause little, if any, problem. A massive increase in quantity or a moved in date many weeks less than the quoted product Lead Time resulted in many problems."

"Just as we did earlier, let's look at a planning system report. Looking at the material planning system (next page) re-enforces the concept. On *11/8/96* one customer asked for an addition to existing schedules of 400 units for delivery in five weeks 12/13/96. Assume:"

- "The shippable product has a Bill of Materials with only one purchased component."
- "The single component is used on many other products."
- "The component has a quoted Lead Time of six (6) weeks."
- "The product quoted Lead Time is based on a component vendor quoted Lead Time of six (6) weeks, which cannot be improved on, plus a manufacturing Cycle time of two (2) weeks."
- "There is no manufacturing capacity constraint to meeting the buyer's request."
- "The material planning system for the component shows:" I put up a slide:

146 • David P. Zimmerman

	Vendor quoted Lead Time of 6 weeks (30 days FIRM). Buy policy (stocking strategy) of 8 weeks (40 days).			
Date	Demand	Supply	Inventory	Comment
11/2/96			396	On-Hand
11/2/96	200		196	Safety Stock
11/8/96	150		46	Planned Requirement
11/14/96		1886	1932	Planned open order receipt
11/15/96	196		1736	Planned Requirement
11/22/96	225		1511	Planned Requirement
11/29/96	360		1151	Planned Requirement
12/6/96	300		851	Planned Requirement
12/13/96	250		601	Planned Requirement
12/20/96	196		405	Planned Requirement
12/27/96	206		199	Planned Requirement

"As we determined earlier, material does exist to meet the buyer request. In our last example, we added the safety stock (200 units) back into the reported available inventory to equal available inventory. But the customer wants to increase schedules by 400 units. That will consume more than our safety stock quantity. We need to look further."

"To calculate the inventory quantity available to meet that request, one looks foreword in time to the vendor quoted Lead Time for the item being purchased. How much inventory is available (the material is needed by manufacturing on 11/29/96)?"

"In my example, 6 weeks Lead Time means 400 units, if ordered 11/9/96, would be received from the vendor 12/20/96. Since 405 units (in addition to safety stock) are in inventory on that date the answer to the request must be yes."

Date	Demand	Supply	Inventory	Comment	Excess
	Vendor quoted Lead Time of 6 weeks (30 days FIRM). Buy policy (stocking strategy) of 8 weeks (40 days).
11/2/96			396	On-Hand	
11/2/96	200		196	Safety Stock	
11/9/96	150		46	Planned Requirement	405
11/14/96		1886	1932	Open buy receipt	199
11/16/96	196		1736	Planned Requirement	0
11/23/96	225		1511	Planned Requirement	1978
11/30/96				Message on buyers report	1722
11/30/96	360		1151	Planned Requirement	1722
12/7/96	300		851	Planned Requirement	1407
12/14/96	250		601	Planned Requirement	1107
12/21/96	196		405	Planned Requirement	857
12/28/96	206		199	Planned Requirement	661
1/4/97	199		0	Planned Requirement	455

"In others a word, the answer to the buyer is yes because the stocking policy forces excess material into inventory. The inventory consumed now is excess inventory not needed until 12/21. That need date exceeds the material quoted Lead Time so the current schedules remain valid and achievable."

"The quantity of excess inventory is a moving target dependent on when, in the order cycle, we take a picture. But here is the general rule: "For planning purposes, I will use an average of ½ buy quantity (stocking strategy) as the definition of how much excess inventory is available at all times."

"When I put that general rule into practice I base quoted Lead Time on ½ buy policy, which in this example is 3 weeks, or 15 days of supply. I based the original quoted product quoted Lead Time of 8 weeks on 6 weeks materials Lead Time plus the manufacturing Cycle Time of two weeks. Changing that product quoted Lead Time to three (3) weeks vendor quoted Lead Time plus the manufacturing Cycle Time better reflects the unit's ability to react to change." This example shows that during the three weeks from 11/8/96 to 11/29/96, there is enough inventory to support change. Inventory replacements arrive on 12/20/96, no disruption to preexisting (or other product) schedules occurs because of material shortages."

"I showed in chapter 13 that inventory could be used to reduce Lead Time. The conclusion from what I show above is that all quoted Lead Times, based on product Cycle Times, are overstated by ½ the buy policy of the bill of materials. The inventory is available; why not use it to reduce quoted Lead Times? This results in an immediate reduction in quoted Lead Time with no change in operating procedures. The second result is that the new quoted Lead Time has more credibility than the old. The customer asked me to react inside quoted Lead Time. I did so because I had the inventory to do so. The customer remembers that reaction and "knows" that my quoted Lead Time can be bettered when needed. When I reduce quoted Lead Time based on available planned inventory:"

- "I increase my credibility with my customers."
- "I propagate, within my department, the fact that inventory quantities affect quoted Lead Time length."

"This adjustment needs a name. Since for all practical purposes quoted Lead Time can be reduced by ½ buy policy, I called the new Lead Time "Practical Lead Time". Planners need to have the new quoted Lead Time available, while the planning system needs to use unaltered Lead Times to correctly perform its functions. A simple modification, or addition, to the planning system meets this need. The program creates a bill of materials listing each component/sub-assembly that directly makes up the shippable part. As this slide shows an additional field (Practical Lead Time) records the value of the items quoted Lead Time less ½ your buy policy (stocking strategy) for that specific item."

Item	Quoted Lead Time	Buy policy	Practical Lead Time	Comments
977064	54		54	Product manufacturing Cycle Time
954421	79	20	69	(79 – 20/2) = 69
201109	89	120	29	(89 – 120/2) = 29
220055	69	120	9	(69 – 120/2) = 9
220066	69	120	9	(69 – 120/2) = 9
241471	69	40	49	(9 – 40/2) = 49
321140	72	20	62	(72 – 20/2) = 62
565979	12	40	0	(12 – 40/2) = -8 use 0
976105	89	120	29	(89 – 120/2) = 29
976106	79	120	19	(79 – 120/2) = 19
977069	89	20	79	(89 – 20/2) = 79
173413	79	120	19	(79 – 120/2) = 19
220054	69	40	49	(69 – 40/2) = 49
Total	(54+89)= 143		(54+79)= 133	

"The Product Practical Lead Time (total) is the sum of the longest supplied item's Practical Lead Time plus the manufacturing Cycle Time for the product. Traditional measure would be Manufacturing Cycle Time plus longest component vendor quoted Lead Time or *89* plus 54 days manufacturing Cycle Time equals 143 days."

"The new measure modifies the longest component Lead Time to 79 days and adds manufacturing Cycle Time (54) to equal 133 days."

"The last step is to add the practical Lead Time to the planning system so that planning, sales, and marketing have the information available to share with customers. And, most importantly, PLT provides data to use when calculating the quantity of safety stock needed to support One Day Lead Times."

"Use Practical Lead Time when:"

- ✓ "Product quoted Lead Time equals component Lead Time plus manufacturing Cycle Time, (an adder for capacity flexibility does not negate this method). PLT cannot add value to quoted Lead Times used to support a price/profit goal by restricting supply."
- ✓ "The next link in the supply chain requests a reduction in quoted Lead Times. Every buyer or planner, who has worked in the trenches, knows the process shown above. The result of this knowledge is that they know every quoted Lead Time can be bettered. What they don't know is by how much. Back in Chapter 2, I defined the criteria of Lead Time, i.e. it must be credible, timely, and adhered to. We void these criteria when all parties easily violate quoted Lead Time. PLT puts a limit on easily changed Lead Times. Bettering PLT quoted Lead Times will involve some "pain" expressed in premiums, overtime, or other extra ordinary efforts. The systems credibility grows in all users perception."

Managing Inventory • 151

- ✓ "You have a desire to quickly show a plan for quoted Lead Time improvement. PLT does not change existing operating plans or procedures while demonstrating a commitment to start a Lead Time reduction effort. It buys the vendor some time to plan the more effective steps defined in the next chapters."
- ✓ "You desire to focus vendor quoted Lead Time reduction efforts to those vendors/components that have the greatest affect the total product quoted Lead Time. When the buyers look at this bill of material, they see three long Lead Time components (part numbers 201109, 976105, and 977069). Traditionally the buyer would pursue each of these in an effort to drive down product Lead Time. However, because buy policies create inventory for two (201109 and 976105) canceling out their effect on the product quoted Lead Times, the most effective action results from item addressing 977069."
- ✓ "You want to formally demonstrate the effect of inventory on Lead Time. I have spent a good deal of time and space showing what many intuitively know, "Inventory affects ones ability to respond to change". PLT systematizes and reinforces this fact in all the minds and practices of all users."

"Now before you ask, PLT is not a numbers game. PLT is a first step in a compensation program that allows vendors to reduce quoted Lead Times while educating their buyers and planners on the relationship between inventory and quoted Lead Time. PLT helps buyers and planners understand the relationship between product Cycle Time, inventory, and Lead Time. Moreover, and most importantly, it provides a data base that will be used later on the path to One Day Lead Times."

"I used this method of determining product quoted Lead Time for over three years without negatively affecting the service level of the supplying organization. It also was used to minimize calculated safety stock requirements for Adaptive Master Scheduling (Chapter 15) and Item Level Mater Scheduling (Chapter 16). Let me summarize"

Practical Lead Time

Strong Points	Weak Points
Quick quoted Lead Time reduction.	No change in component Lead Times.
Drives home, within the supplying organization, the fact that excess inventory quantities directly affect Lead Time length.	Requires software to create useable reports automatically.
Prioritizes Lead Time reduction efforts of buyers.	May be interpreted as a numbers game played by buyers and/or planners.

"This first step reinforced in planning, purchasing, and sales, the effect of inventory on quoted Lead Times. It also serves to make the quoted Lead Time more credible with the customer. Alone, however, its effect on inventory and responsiveness did not match the effect of my goal, One Day quoted Lead Time."

Chapter 15

SAFETY STOCK CALCULATION

"OK Bill" I started, "let's get down to the nitty-gritty. You stated you do not want your buyer to increase inventory and that is a valid point (your point 5). I have shown that you already have more inventory than you plan to have because of vendor Lead Time lengths. The questions now are:"

"What quantity of inventory do I need to quote my customers buyers One Day Lead Time?"
"Is that quantity greater than my current inventory?"
"What are the costs of the inventory?"

"The answers are derived in two stages just as inventory exists in two states, raw materials and finished goods. Each of these states defines the quantity of inventory based on two facts, replenishment time and the magnitude of demand change during the replenishment time. These are the key to inventory management. The old way determined inventory quantity based on attempting to insure we did not shut the line down; we guesstimated the quantity of inventory needed. Now we will use empirically defined inventory quantities. Now we will manage inventory. We will calculate the quantity for each stage, raw materials and finished goods, using the same statistical model.
"The issue I need to address is; who holds the safety stock. Here there are only two options, the vendor or the buyer. I need to know the answer in order to calculate replenishment time, the amount of time that elapses from

the point when I recognize a need until that need is satisfied. If I am the vendor, then:"

> "REPLENISHMENT TIME is the greater of:"
> - "Production frozen zone (to be defined in chapter 16) or,"
> - "Product Practical Lead Time defined as the longest quoted Practical Lead Time for raw materials (Vendor quoted Lead Time less ½ buy policy), plus product Cycle Time for finished product. Since buy policies create inventory, calculating safety stock on the total vendor quoted Lead Time or product Cycle Time would lead to additional excess inventory, double counting."

Mary was right on top of me, "What with this replenishment time and how is it different from Lead Time?"

"Great question Mary," I replied. "Replenishment time I just defined as a calculation much as Cycle Time is the result of a calculation. Lead Time is the result of a business decision, not a calculation. Let me continue and if you still have a problem I'll keep going until I satisfy you questions."

"If I am a buyer then:"

"REPLENISHMENT TIME is the Practical Lead Time of the item I am purchasing (the Lead Time quoted to me by my vendor less ½ my stocking strategy). This definition is straight foreword, however the first needs an example for clarification (coming shortly)."

"The issue I must address is; how often can I accept a stock out? If your answer is never, then you cannot store the amount of safety stock required to support your needs. Never means no conceivable act of God or man would interfere with my service level. That would require an infinite amount of all materials. That, I submit, is unreasonable. Your service level expectation must be set somewhere lower than never."

"Before I go any further, does anybody have a problem with my last statement?"

"Yes Tom."

"What exactly are you saying? That your system cannot improve service or that no system can improve service or what?"

"I'm saying 'or what.' I'm saying that if anyone expects that their vendor to guarantee service regardless of any act of God, or act of man, that person needs to re-examine reality. As an example: My friend's mother recently moved to North Carolina from upstate New York. That winter, North Carolina received four inches of snow in a single day. The town she moved to shut down. They did not have the snow removal equipment to keep up. In Rochester, we consider four inches of snow a dusting; in North Carolina, it's a major storm. Now, in order to protect the residents should the town in North Carolina invest in the kind, and quantity, of snow removal equipment as Rochester? No. We must accept the fact that some risks are acceptable. In the case of safety stock quantities, I use history as the guide to acceptable risk. History reveals itself as forecast accuracy and past buyer performance over replenishment time."

"Example of vendor replenishment time (buyer examples are in the next Chapter):"

"If a component I purchase has a Practical Lead Time of twelve (12) weeks, and my finished product has a manufacturing Cycle Time of two weeks, how much inventory must I carry to give my customers buyer a One Day quoted Lead Time? Here is another way looking at the question. What quantity of safety stock is necessary to eliminate vendor quoted Lead Time and manufacturing Cycle Time as factors in meeting changes in the buyers' demands? When the forecast quantity equals actual (the exact quantities and dates of consumption match perfectly) there is no need for safety stock. If one looked only one week into the future, the magnitude of a demand change over what was forecasted would be much less than one who looks 12, 20 or 36 weeks into the future. We know that actual and forecast seldom match when the time span between forecast and actual need is long."

"The answer to that question lies in the time frames just mentioned and the desired level of service. The desired level of service is the percentage of time that we predict we will successfully meet a One Day quoted Lead Time. That is, in the 14 weeks and the service level desired (say 99.7% or six-sigma repeatability)."

"Take your pencils and write the quantity of safety stock you think would be required to be 99% certain that inventory will be available when a buyer wants it (to support One Day quoted Lead Time) given a Practical Lead Time for raw materials of 12 weeks, and your manufacturing cycle time of eight weeks, and buyer demand is forecast to be between thirty and fifty per week. I'll wait while you write your number."

"Finished" I asked. "Here is my answer. The quantity needed to achieve buyer satisfaction, or to avoid production line outs, is the statistical difference between what was forecast and the actual need at delivery time. Forecast error calculation is the key to understanding safety stock quantities."

"First collect historical data and calculate the standard deviation of the forecast error. Your planning system will tell you the forecasted and actual quantities over the replenishment time product Cycle Time, i.e. 12 weeks material practical Lead Time plus 8 week manufacturing Frozen zone (use the frozen zone when it is greater than manufacturing Cycle Time). The first example below states that on 7/17 the forecasted need for delivery on 12/5 (20 week Lead Time) was 40 units. The actual need on 12/5 was also 40 units. Be careful to record the buyer need, not what was provided (manufactured)."

"Next subtract the forecasted quantity from the actual demand at ship date."

"Then square the delta."

"Sum the squares."

"Lastly calculate the standard deviation using the sum of squares formula."

I put up a slide as a guide.

Vendor	Company A				
Product	9B9740				
Lead time	20 Weeks (100 Days)				

	Forecast		Actual	Delta (1) - (2)	Delta^2
Start Date	Forecast Qty (1)	For a Need Date of	Required Qty (2)		
7/17	40	12/5	40	0	0
7/24	42	12/14	31	-11	121
7/31	37	12/21	42	5	25
8/7	38	12/28	40	2	4
8/14	42	1/5	42	0	0
8/21	51	1/12	45	-6	36
8/29	45	1/19	50	5	25
9/5	30	1/26	45	15	225
9/12	41	2/2	40	-1	1
			Sum of Delta^2		437

S = Sum of Squares 437   N = Number of entries 9   R = Square root of S/N-1

$$\sqrt{\frac{\text{Sum of Square}}{\text{Number of entries - 1}}} = \sqrt{\frac{437}{9-1}} = 7.49$$

"One standard deviation is 7.49 units. Notice that in collecting the data forecast errors I recorded both positive and negative variations. Is inventory needed when the actual demand is less than forecasted demand? No, but the information provides data about bias, if any, and yields a more accurate inventory quantity."

"Now I said that I wanted to be 99% confident that I would meet the demand. 99% is close to three (3) standard deviations. Three standard deviations equals (7.49 * 3) or 22.5 units. Vendor buy policy provides inventory ½ the time so I reduce the inventory required to by ½ or 1.5 standard deviations or 12 units. Compare twelve units to whatever quantity you determined would be needed to be 99% confident that demand would be satisfied for a unit with a twenty week Lead Time."

I watched the smiles as I looked around the room. I decided to let it go rather than ask what quantities they had recorded. I knew from experience that they had recorded between 30 and 50 units. I continued.

"A couple of more facts about forecast error and demand fluctuation in a supply chain. All units within a supply chain have constrained output, hence constrained demand. Constrained output means that any given link has a finite amount of capital equipment, manufacturing space, and resources that create output. The buyer and the vendor must determine what degree of constraint they are working with. A vendor with two production lines shifts all non-capital resources to one product from another to meet demands shifts. That vendor's degree of constraint is less than the vendor who, with the same non-capital manufacturing resources produces only one product at a time. No unit within a supply chain gains or loses capital equipment or non-capital resource quickly. It takes time to ramp up or down a manufacturing operation. Therefore, the degree of demand change is finite. Yet, you and I have seen demand change requests that are several orders of magnitude from each other caused by high inventories that in turn are caused by long Lead Times. Does it sound like I'm repeating myself? I am."

"Now what about consumer demand that is not constrained as are manufacturing vendors?"

DISTRIBUTION "I support end user responsiveness the same way. Use the same formula to calculate safety stock quantities at the distribution level. Example: Lets say that sales and marketing conclude that 100 units of finished product must be available for sale at all times to cover for demand swings. Sales and marketing submit orders to final assembly based on their own actual use. They also provide a forecast of future use. Final assembly maintains a frozen zone equal to their quoted Lead Time. Distribution meets consumer/buyer demands from a combined stock of 100 units plus last delivery from final assemble plus safety stock calculated as shown above, i.e. safety stock quantity based on the forecast error over the final assembly's Lead Time. The final assembly unit could hold the inventory instead of the distribution unit and accomplish the same ends but I prefer that the inventory be kept in one location where feasible."

"Now that we know how to calculate the amount of inventory needed to support One Day Lead Times the next step is to reduce quoted Lead Times and buyer inventory quantities. Remember that the combination of Lead Time length and buyer inventory drive historical forecast error. Both must be reduced. We now have One Day Lead Times. We know how to calculate the quantity of finished goods needed to support that Lead Time. Next, we determine where the inventory is to be located in the supply chain, and how that affects production scheduling."

Degree of accuracy

"Many excellent papers have been written that provide formula for calculation of safety stock quantities. These may be used in place of my admittedly simplistic approach to manage inventory to a finer degree. I avoid a higher degree of forecast error calculation accuracy because doing so implies a greater degree of control than reality shows. Suffice to say that a high degree of control implies a highly reactive supply chain. A highly reactive supply chain implies a high quantity of transactional activity between links within the chain. One of my goals is to reduce transactional activity so that the supply chain is managed as opposed to a supply chain that simply reacts to change. To meet that goal I use the more simplistic inventory calculation."

"Now that we know how to calculate a safety stock quantity it is time to systemically use that safety stock in support of One Day quoted Lead Times. That will allow us to effectively define how much we save with One Day Lead Times. Remember, Bill wants no added inventory and, he wants good service. I'll address the service next but for now please note that the safety stock calculation yields a quantity of inventory less than your current quantities. This fact I will build on as we progress."

Chapter 16

ADAPTIVE MASTER SCHEDULING (AMS)

"Let's keep building. We know that a controlled, read empirically defined, quantity of inventory supports One Day Lead Times. We know how to calculate the amount of safety stock required to meet our buyer's needs (empirically define). We know that loading that quantity of safety stock into our planning system will not facilitate One Day Lead Times. So how, in our planning system, do we use the safety stock quantity we just learned how to calculate?"

"Adaptive Master Scheduling (AMS) modifies the production planning system so that safety stock (finished goods inventory) is controlled while smoothing production schedules. While a retailer satisfies buyers with inventory only, AMS satisfies buyers using normal build schedules and filling any extra demand from safety stock. The retailer shields the consumer from product Cycle Times as AMS shields the buyer from product Cycle Times. The major differences lie in the empirical quantification of inventory quantities and the ability of AMS to monitor inventory, reducing production schedules when demand does not meet forecasts, and increasing schedules when required. AMS is a compensating technique whose value (defined as the quantity of safety stock required to support One Day Lead Times) decreases as Cycle Times are reduced. Keeping finished goods inventory at the vendor reduces the total amount of inventory of finished goods in the supply chain because the buyer does keep hedge inventory to compensate for long Lead Times. It removes the need for inventory at the buyer's site. The total amount of finished goods equals the sum of the buyers' inventories (as raw material) plus the vendor's inventory. The amount of raw material inventory carried by each buyer is proportional to the Lead Time quoted by each vendor. Reduce the quoted Lead Time, and the buyer's need for raw material inventory goes down, thus the total quantity of inventory decreases."

"AMS is a software addition to a production planning system that modifies production quantities using an algorithm that includes an averaging of demand (a smoothing technique). It meets customer needs with production quantities. If, and when, the quantity produced is less than customer needs safety stock fills that need. The algorithm supports One Day Quoted Lead Times with finished goods inventory (the safety stock). It is a tool that allows the vendor to quote One Day Lead Times and deliver on that quote because it overrides the logic errors of our planning systems and uses safety stock as it has always been intended. Once One Day Lead Times become the norm, everyone reaps its advantages. Before I get into more detail a quick review of the advantages is in order."

I wrote on my chart paper. *Reduced inventory quantities,* and continued. "A buyer receives One Day Quoted Lead Times when the vendor agrees to hold finished goods inventory for the buyer. That means that the buyer's stocking strategy defines his/her inventory quantities (inventory equals one-half stocking strategy). This results in the vendor, using the method shown in Chapter 15 to calculate finished goods inventory quantities (safety stock), minimizing finished goods inventory. Add to that ½ buy policy (stocking strategy) inventory for the buyer, equals total inventory quantities. Now Bill, when you compare that total to the inventory currently held by your buyers you will find it is less than the combined inventory quantities generated by both under longer quoted Lead Times (the calculations shown in Chapter 11)."

"NOTE: Yes, as a vendor, you should know your buyers stocking strategy and average inventory quantities of your product(s). That knowledge allows you to sell the advantages of One Day Lead Times."

Next, I wrote *Reduced transactional activity.* "Less inventory at the buyers means that the vendor's frequency of open order maintenance disappears because the buyer no longer attempts to control his/her inventory through changes to open orders (it may in fact mean that there are less open orders). However, the One Day Lead Time implies that the manufacturing unit has the flexibility and capability to change as required by the buyer. Adaptive Master Scheduling insures flexibility."

Lastly, I wrote *Smoother production (manufacturing) operations.* "Adaptive Master Scheduling is a technique that modifies production planning systems to systemically monitor safety stock quantities, so that they neither grow or become totally depleted while protecting the manufacturing operation from drastic schedule changes and meeting buyer needs. Adding Adaptive Master Scheduling to the production control software insures low cost order maintenance in support of the One Day quoted Lead Time."

"*Back to AMS*. I said at the outset that AMS is a software add-on to the production planning system. That is just a little simplistic. AMS is software, but it is also a way of running a manufacturing unit. Like Master Scheduling, it creates production frozen zones to protect the manufacturing unit from short-term change (the results of all calculations become effective outside this zone). Because of demand averaging, it protects against extreme quantity changes. Because each calculation monitors safety stock quantities, it guards against stock outs and excess inventories. Because it does all this quickly, it improves vendor's service while buying the time to conduct root cause analysis and Cycle Time reduction programs that takes longer. The key to AMS lies in the proper calculation of safety stock quantities and the systemic inclusion of that quantity in the manufacturing strategy of the user. Last chapter I addressed the safety stock quantities, now I add manufacturing strategy. I define manufacturing strategy in terms of a production frozen zone and a demand-averaging zone."

"This is in your handouts so no need to write it down," I said. "The AMS formula is:"

Build quantity = Average demand + Safety Stock adjustment + Manufacturing constraint

Where:

Average demand = Sum of all buyer demands over the Averaging zone / Averaging zone
Safety Stock adjustment = Current or forecasted inventory quantity − Calculated Safety Stock quantity
Manufacturing Constraint = Appropriate factor to meet your Minimum lot size, EOQ, or lot size multiple

---

"Those components used by the AMS algorithm are:" I clicked them off as I wrote.

Buyer forecasted needs, Production frozen zone, Production averaging zone, Calculated Safety Stock quantities, and Manufacturing constraints.

I then pointed at each as I explained.

"*Buyer forecasted needs* Your customer's buyer must agree to provide, on a regular basis (at least monthly), a forecast of their expected requirements for your product. The time period covered by the forecast must not be less than your total product Cycle Time (Longest purchased component quoted Lead Time plus your manufacturing Cycle Time). The frequency of updates to the forecast must not be less than the shorter of your shipping frequency or manufacturing frequency. Included in the forecast, the buyer must share their current inventory quantities of your product(s). CAUTION: Do not be concerned with the accuracy of the forecast; remember forecast error helps you define safety stock quantities. You must reassure your buyers that the forecast they provide is not a tool you use to beat them up, or hold them financially liable, it is a tool used to help support One Day Lead Times. However, you as the vendor expect the forecast your buyers provides to be their best estimate of needs. With calculated forecast error, you can see if the forecast bias exists. If bias exists then the buyer must, contractually, accept financial responsibility for the bias amount."

"*Production frozen zone* A frozen zone is the first element of your manufacturing strategy. This is the amount of time, defined by your production group (manufacturing unit), during which AMS software cannot change previously calculated production quantities. If buyer demand decreased during the frozen zone, the excess production becomes inventory (The formula above reduces future production quantities because inventory quantities increase). That is how the formula controls inventory insuring it does not grow out of control.). If demand exceeds the production quantity, the additional quantity comes from safety stock (Again, in the formula above increases future production quantities because inventory is less than desired. That is how the formula controls inventory insuring it does not shrink out of control.). AMS software overrides planning system calculated build quantities and replaces them with previously calculated build quantities during the frozen zone. Outside the frozen zone AMS enters into the planning system its own calculated production build quantities based on the formula."

"*Production averaging zone* The second element of your manufacturing strategy, this production smoothing technique averages the number of weeks, or days, of buyer demand quantities you define. Each base production quantity equals the average of the total forecasted demand during the average zone. The greater the number of weeks included the less effect production "bumps" have on the average. However, the greater the number of weeks in the average zone the greater the average amount of inventory carried (I'll share an example later in the Details section)."

"*Safety Stock quantities* Are the quantity defined by the safety stock calculation."

"*Manufacturing constraints* The third element of your manufacturing strategy is any other factor, defined by the manufacturing unit, that defines production quantities, i.e. lot size multiples, economic order quantities, or minimums."

Summary

"As shown in this slide AMS combines the discipline of an MRP master scheduling process with the need to be responsive to buyer needs. The technique quickly reduces inventory levels and improves vendor responsiveness; it does not optimize either. The process leaves component Lead Times as is; instead, it concentrates on customer service while reducing production planning activities and inventory levels. AMS answers Bill last point in that it insure vendor responsiveness."

AMS	
Strong Points	Weak Points
Implemented across full product or buyer base.	Inventory is in high cost finished goods
Reduces total supply chain inventory • Minimizes the magnitude of changes in manufacturing quantities. • Reduces inventory risk for buyers. • Allows smoother distribution of product to meet the varying needs of buyers.	Most inventory is at the vendors.
Quick improvement in buyer relations.	Short-term buyer anxiety over perceived risk exposure.
Averaging in manufacturing smoothes demand variability to component vendors.	Hides true problem of vendors' Lead Time length.
Buys vendors time to attack true Lead Time drivers and Cycle Time.	Does not attack Cycle Time.
Requires long-term commitments between buyer and vendor.	Requires long-term commitments between buyer and vendor.

The Details

The information that follows is not part of the presentation above.

Implementation of One Day quoted Lead Times using Adaptive Master Scheduling requires a plan. The steps in the plan are (you are the vendor, your customers are the buyers):

1. Define current state and associated costs (Set your baseline).
2. Define the buyer(s) you will work with (do not try to do all at once; start up takes resources).
3. Calculate the amount of safety stock required by product, by buyer.
4. Define internal production strategy.
5. Agree internally to the process (production, planning, sales, and purchasing) and get management buy-in.
6. Commit you and your buyer to the process (communicate).
7. Modify internal systems as necessary
8. Initiate (move inventory from buyer to you).
9. Track and report, internally, results.
10. Plan for the next phase (Chapter 17).

1. Define current state.

Base lines form the starting point of any improvement program and quantify the return on investment. Our baseline consists of these elements.

> ➤ *Sales transactional activity costs* The cost of open order maintenance including sales, production planning expedites and de-expedites. The goal is zero.
> ➤ *Inventory costs* The vendor's current finished goods inventory, if any, and the buyer's current raw material inventory of the vendor's product(s). The goal for the latter is one-half buyers buy policy.

Example: when I introduced this program to one buyer our base was:

Lead Time = 200 days,

The buyer's buy policy was monthly (20 working days), and

The buyer's current inventory of my product was two months supply (about 200 units).

The result:

I calculated safety stock at 50 units (using the method in Chapter 15),

The buyer changed her buy policy to weekly.

The total inventory between the buyer and me – 60 units or a reduction of 140 units (200 – 60) at $1500 per unit equals $210,000 inventory reduction.

NOTE: If the buyer had not reduced her buy policy, the total inventory would have been 100 units (1/2 buy policy = 50 units + my safety stock of 50 units) for a $150,000 inventory reduction.

2. Assign buyers/products implementation priority

The people who will be responsible for the One Day Lead Time program need to define their current circumstances or environment. Each organization is both buyer (from vendors both internal and external) and vendor to the next link in the supply chain. Both vendor and buyer require databases that meet their specific needs.

- *Vendors* (sales and production)
    - Define which buyers/products are the biggest in terms of sales volume.
    - Collect historical data to form a base line by buyer/product:
        - Current quoted Lead Times to these buyers by product sold,
        - Your current finished goods inventory levels (both internal, if any, and at the buyers site), and
        - Sales transactional activity on open order maintenance
    - Set up central data base to track costs/savings.
- *Buyers*
    - Insure that vendor quoted Lead Times are accurate.
    - Begin to collect data on vendor Lead Time costs.
        - Your raw material inventory quantities measured in dollars and days of supply.
        - Transactional costs for open order maintenance (include expedites and deexpedites or cancellation requests).
        - Cost of vendor non-acceptance (include expedites and deexpedites or cancellations).

The products/buyers chosen for implementation of the Lead Time reduction program need only be willing to adopt the new process i.e. be willing to accept One Day quoted Lead Times and reduced inventories. The reason we wanted to know the biggest was to determine who would be approached first so they, and we, could get the greatest benefit. The longest Lead Time quoted will yield the biggest return in terms of savings and service.

3. Calculate safety stock quantities

Using the formula from Chapter 14, calculate the safety stock required that support a One Day quoted Lead Time by product. Use aggregate buyer demand forecasts and actual demand to calculate the demand.

This process may represent a major change in your thinking. Demand means what the buyer wants, not what you are willing to sell. If you use lot size minimums, or multiples, to increase demand those numbers may not be used to calculate safety stock levels. Remember that order minimums and multiples only increases the inventory of the buyer in terms of days of supply, which converts into more changes to open orders.

Next, convert demand to weekly (if not daily) requirements. Longer periods may be used temporarily if transportation costs are excessive. Longer-term alternate plans need to be in place so that the transportation issue is neutralized. When data does not exist, average demands downward to weekly buckets (if only monthly demands exist, divide that demand quantity by 4.3).

> *Transportation* At one point in my career I dealt with a long supply chain (Guadalajara Mexico, to upstate New York). Since the transportation Cycle Time exceeded my desired One Day Lead

Time, I protected my buyer by keeping all safety stock not in the manufacturing area, Guadalajara, but at the buyer's site. I maintained financial responsibility and ownership of the inventory and showed a buyer location for the quantity at that site in my local (Guadalajara) planning system. The buyer was happy to supply the inventory information in exchange for the reduced Lead Time. Before you ask, lets summarize what that means.

$ Where One Day Lead Times exist, long transportation Cycle Times equals increased product Cycle Times equals more safety stock (since safety stock quantities are based on forecast error which is based on time, i.e. the longer the forecast time period the greater the probability and magnitude of forecast error). The greater the quantities of safety stock the greater the risk of scrap to the manufacturer (vendor). Alternatively, where One Day Lead Times do not exist excess inventory exists (remember excess inventory is equal to the quantity of inventory above ½ stocking strategy inventory).

$ This means that a link in a supply chain can now calculate total cost of their long supply chain as the purchase price of item plus the cost of the increased safety stock quantity needed to support One Day Lead Times. Again, where One Day Lead Times do not exist, total costs equals the price of the item plus the cost of excess inventory.

4. Define internal production strategy

The manufacturing arm (production) defines an averaging zone, a frozen zone, and production frequency.

NOTE: Since I never say never and always avoid always, it follows that frozen production can be changed in the case of an emergency. I base the plan and all calculations on the assumption that the production schedule will not change during the frozen period.

This step accomplishes four things for organizations that are not involved in continuous production (continuous production areas skip this step):

- Increase quality.
- Shelter production from short term expediting.
- Help maintain safety stock levels.
- Free up resources to work on manufacturing Cycle Time reduction.

The *production frequency* is how often a production lot is manufactured. We defined the production lots releases to be weekly because:

- ➢ Increased Cycle of Learning from consistent repetition of the same job. Operators, set up personnel, inspectors and testers did not require as large a start up time because they remembered each job. The learning curve is one of the definers of actual cost of manufacturing.
- ➢ Increased quality because the smaller lot sizes meant errors, if any, were found quickly and corrective action taken for the next release. Releases that are more frequent meant that the Cycle of Learning increased driving quality levels up.

> Increased attention to Cycle Time reduction efforts as the "fixed" cost per lot were highlighted.

The *averaging zone* defines the number of weeks (or days) aggregated buyer demand that is averaged. If, in consultation with the production group, I determine I do not want production quantities to vary more than 10%, the averaging period used to determine production quantities would be 10 runs. 5% would be 20 runs and 20% would be 5 runs. Example, when normal production is in weekly buckets and a 20% change is acceptable, the demands for the next 5 weeks are averaged (total divided by 5). The result is the production schedule for week one of 5. The schedule for week two totals the demand for weeks 2 through 6, and then divides by 5, etc.

Week	1	2	3	4	5	6	7	8	9	10
Demand	20	40	30	50	20	40	40	60	50	30
2 week average	30	35	40	35	30	40	50	55	40	
4 week average	35	35	35	38	40	48	45			
6 week average	34	37	40	43	40					
8 week average	38	42	40							
10 week average	38									

Production leveling using this technique becomes an element of your manufacturing strategy based on the amount of manufacturing quantity fluctuation you want relative to demand fluctuation.

The *frozen zone* is the amount of time, defined by the production group, during which production schedules (quantity and timing) cannot be changed. If buyer demand decreased during the frozen zone the excess production would be kept with safety stock (see step 7 for details). If demand exceeded the production, the additional quantity comes from safety stock. Each time a calculation is done, the weeks specified are frozen, any changes occur after the frozen period.

Modify internal planning system

If a safety stock of 12 units was calculated to satisfy forecasted demands shown below, and the calculating zone were 8 weeks, and there was no frozen zone, the build scheduled projected would be as shown (no allowance for run multiples or minimums are included).

Date	Inv.	1/2	1/9	1/9	1/16	1/23	1/30	2/7	2/14	2/21	2/28	3/7
Demand		40	50	30	45	38	37	40	41	48	35	36
Supply		39	48	39	39	39						
Projected Inv.	15	14	12	21	15	16						

Manufacturing order for 1/2 is:
Σ Demand 8 weeks/8 +(calculated safety stock - current inv.)/frozen zone or
(40+50+30+45+38+37+40+41)/8 + (12-15)/8.

The next week follows the same thought process and assumes the forecasted need would be consumed.

(50+30+45+38+37+40+41+48)/8 + (12-14)/8 (the algorithm compensates for spikes to insure that the ideal safety stock quantity is not at risk). This process has been in use for three years (as of this writing) resulting in inventory reduction, smooth production schedules and improved buyer relations. These improvements resulted in a quoted Lead Time reduction from 200 days to 1 day. My customer had kept eight weeks of inventory as a hedge against schedule changes; I needed 12 units as a safety stock against change. They guessed; I calculated.

With the use of AMS, the fluctuation in manufacturing orders (supply) becomes less than the actual demand change. Relative smoothness comes from averaging all figures. The degree of smoothness depends on the length of the calculating zone.

The vendor now knows the quantity of safety stock they will need (that information will be shared with the buyer), and what the manufacturing strategy will be. Safety stock strategies cannot reduce total inventories and costs unless the next link in the supply chain reduces their inventory. The buyer's input and concerns must be addressed. The vendor shares, with the buyer, the goal of reducing total inventories, and increasing responsiveness. The buyer agrees to reduce their inventory of your product as you reduce your quoted Lead Time to One Day.

5. Reach internal consensus

At this point data should exist that shows the advantages of the proposed process.

- Proposed safety stock levels (costs) have been determined.
- Current finished goods inventory levels are defined (your and the buyer(s)).
- Open order transactional activity is known.
- Effects on production scheduling and planning transactional activities are known.

This data will show that the vendors costs are reduced in total because increased finished goods inventory carrying costs are offset by:

- $ Reduced transactional activity.
- $ Reduced (elimination) of overtime to meet unforecasted demands.

- $ Reduced (elimination) of premium charges for raw materials ordered to meet unforecasted demands. Vendor relationships improve because short-term open order changes are reduced (if production schedules are frozen, the orders for materials to support production is also frozen).
- $ Improved quality because of smoother planning (fewer rush orders).
- $ Improved ability to reduce costs through Cycle Time reduction.
- $ Improved competitive advantage because of your ability to react to any change without Lead Time restrictions.
- $ Improved buyer relations as buyer inventories are reduced.

These results are only the start. Additional savings will be realized when these concepts are included in the raw material purchasing arena (Chapter 17).

6. *Buyer involvement*

Buyer contacts begin with the introduction of the relationships between Lead Time length and costs. Teams visit buyers and define the savings that each will realize when Lead Times are reduced. A presentation must include an honest exchange of information such as the current buy policies of the buyer and the current inventory levels for the items under discussion. At the conclusion, the buyer must agree (contractually) to a set of rules that must be adhered to if they are to gain the advantages of very short Lead Times. The rules (*and logic*) are:

> Buyer inventory levels must be reduced to one week's worth of each item. *Controlling inventory*

levels is the biggest single reason for change. As the next link in the supply chain changes demand, each preceding link attempts to react. When inventory exceeds short-term need, the flow of new materials is cut off (Chapter 6). Because the buyers' on hand inventory is so much greater than the calculated safety stock level, the inventory reduction program can be complicated. In one extreme case the circuit board assembly area cut their production rate in half for three months to allow the buyer to consume their excess inventory. Each week's buyer demand was met 50% from new production, 50% from on hand inventories.

➢ The buyer agrees to provide a rolling demand forecast covering the vendors' product Cycle time, updated monthly. The vendor agrees that the forecast accuracy is not an issue. *The vendors Cycle Time has not changed, AMS only compensates for the effects of long Lead Times. The long-term solution is short Lead Times supported by short Cycle Times. Forecast accuracy is not an issue because the forecast error defines safety stock level that compensates for the forecast errors.* However, forecast bias is not forecast error and must not be allowed. *Forecast bias is forecast error that is consistently higher (or lower) than actual demand. Its result is to force vendors to carry unofficial safety stock for buyers.*

I know of some buyers who, to protect themselves from all possible error, provide vendors with forecasts that always exceed their actual need. They try to create safety stock without accepting liability for error. They define Win-Win as "I win twice". Such a buyer cannot be involved in Lead Time management because this buyer practices Lead Time manipulation. Biasing forecast error in this manner forces excess inventory into the supply chain just as vendor long quoted Lead Times did. Because the vendor now holds the inventory, the buyer feels secure in knowing he/she did a good job

Sorry, but that kind of thought process, let alone practice, will not fly for long. A long-term relationship cannot exist in an environment where one side attempts to take advantage of the other. Remember, competitive advantages support price/profit; they do not, effectively, support excess inventory. The vendor needs safety stock to respond to demand changes when an actual demand exceeds the forecasted demand. Inventory caused by bias can never be used because the forecast continually exceeds what will happen. How do I know when bias exists? The formula (F-a)/n defines the degree of bias. Since bias can be calculated, the resultant inventory costs can be allocated based on the calculation back to the buyer. My contract with

$$\text{Bias} = \frac{\text{Forecast demand - actual demand}}{\text{SampleSize}}$$

buyers stated that the buyer was responsible for the full cost of any inventory that resulted from forecast bias as well as the carrying cost for that inventory. If the buyer continued to bias their forecast, I reduced the calculated safety stock quantity by the bias quantity. *The AMS program systematizes safety stock calculations and negates the perceived need for forecast bias.*

➢ In the event of program cancellation or mandatory design changes, the buyer agrees to be financially responsible for the vendor's safety stock inventory. *A comparison of the current inventory at the buyers*

to the projected safety stock carried at the vendors shows the risk to the buyer is less than prior to AMS. If a program cancellation or mandatory design change existed before AMS, the buyer would be responsible for the entire inventory on site. Since the new safety stock amount is greatly lower than current inventory, the buyer has less risk.
- The vendor agrees not to raise prices to cover the inventory carrying cost of the safety stock. *See above costs.*
- Define a time line for implementation and/or further discussions.

7. Systems

AMS logic is different from existing planning system logic. Changes to apply AMS logic (override planning system logic) must be installed at the vendor. This logic can be homegrown or subcontracted out. The elements of logic are:

- Averaging zone (demand period to be averaged)
- Frozen zone (manufacturing period that, once established, does not change as supply/demand changes).
- The AMS logic is the greater of:
  - Average demand + safety stock replenishment/ averaging period
  - Spike demand + safety stock replenishment/ averaging period

The results of these calculations are tested against manufacturing lot size and lot multiple rules to determine actual manufacturing order quantity.

8. Initiate

All parties to this process begin to exercise their respective responsibilities.

9. Track and report.

The AMS team must track and report to their management actual vs. projected saving/cost as defined in step 1. These figures form the basis for implementation of the next improvement project, Item Level Master Scheduling.

❖

❖

❖

Chapter 17

ITEM LEVEL MASTER SCHEDULING
(ILMS)

"Finished goods inventory (managed by AMS) allowed you, as the vendor, to react quickly to changing buyer demands using finished goods inventory as a buffer. It allows you, as a vendor, to quote One Day Lead Times. As a side benefit, by averaging demand and meeting unforecasted demand changes with buffer, it protects the manufacturing unit (production) from high order of magnitude schedule changes. Quick question – Given the option of finished goods inventory or raw material inventory is finished goods inventory the smartest way to support One Day quoted Lead Times?"

"Depends," volunteered Mary, "on the relative quantity of each. If the total value of finished goods is greater than the value of raw materials then finished goods are cheaper."

"OK" I replied, "but in general terms which?"

Again Mary replied, "All things being equal, raw material inventory is cheaper because its value does not include the labor that finished goods inventory contains."

"That right, as far as it goes," I said "but there is more. Remember the logic I have used all the way through this presentation. Long Lead Times drive not only increased inventory quantities but also drive increased transactional activities. That logic says that when my inventory consists of raw materials I win twice. I'll explain further."

"One Day Lead Times always require some level of finished goods inventory to meet unforecasted demand increases. That's because we have limited capacity. None of us have zero Cycle Times and infinite capacity, but our customers like us to react as if we did. Well, with finished goods inventory we can react as if we have infinite capacity. The trick is to minimize the quantity of finished good inventory. How? The answer lies in the safety stock calculation. More specifically, the answer lies in the period used by the forecast error calculation. *Forecast error = forecasted quantity less actual quantity; where forecasted quantity is a projection of the quantity required at a future date. For finished goods, the future date is the sum of the last operation's Cycle Time plus the longest practical Lead Time in the Bill of Materials. For raw materials, it is the practical Lead Time of the raw material.* Since we know that the product Cycle Time is the base number, reducing product Cycle Time is the key to lowering safety stock quantities (all else being equal). Product Cycle Time is the sum of longest raw material practical Lead Time and manufacturing Cycle Time. Previously I said that the biggest single component of product Cycle Time is vendor quoted Lead Time. Therefore, the key to Cycle Time reduction is reducing vendor Lead Time. If our vendors all quoted One Day Lead Times safety stock calculations would be based on manufacturing Cycle Time plus one day (plus transportation time if needed)."

"Two problems face the buyer as they attempt to reduce vendor quoted Lead Time:"

"First, some vendors will not reduce Lead Times."

"Second, it takes a long time to work through the vendor base reducing each vendor's quoted Lead Times."

"Just as AMS used finished goods inventory to compensate for the combined effects of long vendor Lead Times and manufacturing Cycle Times, Item Level Master Scheduling (ILMS) compensates for long vendor Lead Times. Raw material inventory (safety stock of all purchased items) allows a manufacturer (buyer) to negate the effect of vendor Lead Times thus reducing the quantity of finished goods safety stock required to support One Day quoted Lead Times. ILMS buys the procurement group the time needed to work through their vendor base reducing, where they can, vendor Lead Times, and/or finding vendors willing to work on reducing their quoted Lead Times. Success is measured in terms of total inventory quantities needed to support One Day Lead Times. The result is a reduction of total inventory costs without loss of service."

Bill was red in the face "Are you trying to tell me and my buyers that we need more inventory"

"That all depends on your definition of more," I started. "Let's run through the concept again."

"When you quote One Day Lead Times by holding finished goods inventory, while insisting that your customers hold none, you reduce the total amount of inventory dramatically. Further, you reduce transactional costs in terms of order maintenance and production reschedules at the same time."

"Because those statements are true, it follows that simulating the effects produces the same results. That is to say, when you hold raw material inventory, as safety stock, you force the effect of your vendor quoting One Day Lead Times thus reaping the rewards. The trick is to freeze transactional activity inside your vendors quoted Lead Time. The vendor sees no open order changes, and you insure adequate supply from agreed to delivery schedules and quantities while the safety stock inventory insures available material for changes inside Lead Time. Systemically this means that you may treat all vendor Lead Times as being One Day long. Let me show you how it works and then we will re-examine your concern again."

"We calculate safety stock quantities using the same forecast error formula shown in Chapter 14 substituting vendor practical quoted Lead Time for product Cycle Time. Calculating safety stock quantities the same way for every vendor, based on practical quoted Lead Time, meant that the cost of inventory/product by Lead Time is quantifiable. Quantifiable costs mean that the price of vendor A with Lead Time x (therefore a safety stock cost of $x) when compared to the price of vendor B with Lead Time equal to y (therefore a safety stock cost of $y) yields a total cost figure. I know, and can tell vendors, how much their Lead Time costs me. Vendors can know and communicate to potential buyers how much they save when their quoted Lead Time is lower than a competitor. Lastly, the safety stock, and supporting planning system changes relieved the buyer from transactional activities (open order maintenance) so that they could work with vendors on Lead Time reduction."

"So Bill," I continued, "The inventory quantities, in dollars, continues to shrink. First through Adaptive Master Scheduling, then additional reductions result from Item Level Master Scheduling. You can now tell your vendor, what their Lead Time costs you. You can then point out that when the vendor keeps safety stock you both win. The vendor will see the effects themselves as you use ILMS because they will see a drastic reduction in transactional activity. Test them on it. Each time you see them ask how their sales and order entry people like the reduction in change notices from you. For those vendors who simply say thank you and do not adopt the processes themselves, your only choice is to seek partners that are more cooperative. Meanwhile your inventory and transactional cost are kept to a minimum because you choose to use these processes. Compare this approach to our traditional approach of telling your vendors to keep inventory for you in order to reduce their Lead Time without showing them how to effectively accomplish the task. The first, while in the short term keeping inventory off your books, does not shield you from the cost of ineffective inventory management or eventual inventory liability. It does not share with the vendor how to manage inventory. The One Day Lead Time process limits liability because of reduced inventory quantities, and effectively manages inventory quantities. While you are talking with your vendors about this process, implement the ILMS process at your site(s)"

"The keys to ILMS are safety stock and purchasing planning systems modifications. We have already discussed the safety stock calculation. The purchasing systems modification consists of using the safety stock and delaying replenishment of any used safety stock to outside vendor quoted Lead Time. Remember Chapter 12 where I showed that planning systems do not allow the use of safety stock as designed. To overcome that problem, modify the purchasing planning system by adding software that over rides normal logic inside vendor quoted Lead Time so that as long as total inventory is a positive number no buyer messages appear. Eliminate safety stock as a demand inside vendor Lead Time. Keep safety stock as a demand outside vendor Lead Time. That way, safety stock is available inventory inside Lead Time eliminating buyer messages directing the buyer to replace used safety stock inside vendor Lead Time. Outside vendor quoted, Lead Time normal planning continues."

"The result is a major reduction of open order maintenance and new buy messages inside vendor quoted Lead Time. Safety Stock meets all unforecasted needs, buyer action inside Lead Time becomes unnecessary."

"Now you have an integrated supply chain built into your production planning and materials planning systems. Each vendor and customer has his or her individual idiosyncrasy and proclivity considered as part of the system. The supply chain is not only integrated in terms of communication, the integration is an integral part of the very systems that run your business."

Summary

"As I did in the last chapter I break off here to allow those who do not need the details of implementation to go to the next chapter. First, AMS and ILMS are compensating techniques that involve a broad-brush approach. They work with the vendors and buyers entire database to quickly allow the vendors organization to shelter buyers from the long quoted Lead Times. But they are compensating techniques; they result in higher than necessary levels of inventory. Further efforts are needed to drive inventory levels lower; to support One Day quoted Lead Times. The next chapters assume that the buyer has compensating techniques in place and therefore has the time and tools to address vendors quoted Lead Times more effectively."

ILMS	
Strong Points	Weak Points
Reduces inventory cost by shifting inventory from finished goods to raw materials.	Inventory is higher than desired at the buyer's facility.
Reduces transactional activity for buyers and vendors through the correct use of safety stock by the planning system.	Short term anxiety by buyer due to change in job duties (less expediting more problem solving).
Maintains quick responsiveness to the next level of the supply chain.	Hides true problem of vendor's Lead Time length.
Requires no change on the vendor's part.	Does not attack Cycle Time.
Frees up time, and provides a tool to address quoted lead Times	

Details

These details are not part of the oral presentation above. The steps to implement Item Level Master Scheduling are:

1. Calculate safety stock quantities
2. Modify planning system to accept safety stock correctly
3. Reduce finished goods buffer stock based on new product Cycle Time
4. Work with vendors to reduce their quoted Lead Times.

❖ *Calculate safety stock quantities* for each purchased item using the same formula as used in AMS. First determine the service level desired - I used 97%, because buy policies provided safety stock 50% of the time, so I only needed to cover the other 50%. Therefore, Safety Stock equals 2 times the square root of the sum of forecasted demand (FD) less actual demand (AD) squared over the item's quoted Lead Time divided by the sample size (N) less one. Vendor performance also drives safety stock calculations and must be added to the formula. Vendor performance changes the formula to:

$$SS = 2 * \sqrt{\frac{\Sigma (FD - AD)^2}{N - 1}}$$

$$SS = \left(2 * \sqrt{\frac{\Sigma (FD - AD)^2}{N - 1}} \right) +$$

(average daily demand * average number of delivery days late)

Forecast vs. actual inventory quantities cannot be used because the delta in inventory quantity may have been caused by demand as well as by supply. Therefore, to limit the calculation to supply problems only one needs to track vendor performance in terms of days late per item.

I do not use quantities due vs. actual quantities delivered because those quantities reflect buyer stocking strategies rather than actual needs.

- ❖ *Modify planning System* As I pointed out in Chapter 12, planning systems typically do not allow a buyer to use safety stock as intended. The buying organization's system must be changed. The planning system must use safety stock as it is intend, i.e., allow it to be depleted and stay depleted through the quoted Lead Time of the purchased item. Another way of saying the same thing: Safety stock does not constitute a demand. Total available inventory stays positive until it has been consumed by actual demand, or said another way, until actual demand consumes all available inventory including safety stock.
  - ➤ Add the safety stock quantity to the projected inventory amount. The logic is in addition to the normal planning system logic, not in place of that logic. Do not throw out existing programs, if they consume safety stock; modify them to meet the realities of safety stock.

Managing Inventory • 191

Example

Date	Demand	Supply	Inventory	Actual Inv.	Suggestion	Comment
12/1/96			1351	1351		On-Hand Inventory
12/1/96	200		1151	1351		Safety Stock
12/7/96	300		851	1051		Planned Requirement
12/14/96	250		601	801		Planned Requirement
12/21/96	196		405	605		Planned Requirement
12/28/96	306		99	299		Planned Requirement
1/4/97	199		-100	100	***	Planned Requirement *Message on Buyers report*
1/11/97			1878	2078	1978	Open order receipt

The example above shows a planning system that generates a message to the buyer for 1/4/97 stating the open order due 1/11 should be expedited one week. The new logic would block that buyer message because the safety stock will meet the need (−100 + 200 = 100). Messages that pass the logic, and are forwarded to the buyer when projected inventory less safety stock equals zero or less, i.e. in the example above on the message appears on 1/11/97.

The logic reduces the transactional activities of the buyer and the vendor by suggesting action only when it is mandatory.

❖ *Calculate new safety stock quantities for finished goods.* The effective Lead Time, for purchase items is One Day. The product Cycle Time is now one day plus manufacturing Cycle Time. Use the new answer to calculate a reduced finished goods safety stock level, i.e. forecast quantities at Manufacturing Cycle Time vs. actual demand.

- ❖ *Work with vendors* Now that the buyer no longer spends as much time working the planning system, vendors quoted Lead Times become the priority. Each Item's safety stock level times its carrying cost (inventory cost) equates to its cost of Lead Time.

*Item Lead Time Cost = Safety Stock Quantity * Carrying cost*

Buyers prioritize items by cost then share with the vendors the effects of Lead Time. Vendors learn not only the inventory costs, but also transactional costs, and production interruptions that are the direct result of Lead Time length. In short, section one of this book. Buying organizations then modify quoting and purchased goods cost models to reflect the cost of Lead Time. Vendor's item total cost now consists of the product's unit price plus Lead Time cost. Total cost is used as one variable in vendor selection and retention. Total cost figures provide a negotiating tool that can be used to focus negotiations.

Chapter 18

NEGOTIATING WITH VENDORS

"Buyers, planners, managers all, let us review where we are. Check these off with me:" I put up the slide.

- ❖ **"Lead Time defines when an action needs to take place to insure the timely start of the next dependent action."**
- ❖ **"Lead Time length is the amount of time, defined by a vendor, required to meet a request or demand."**
- ❖ **"Safety stock allows any link in a supply chain to provide One Day Lead Times."**
- ❖ **"Modifying planning systems allows the effective use of the safety stock quantity determined by the product Cycle Time."**

My audience had been quiet for quite a while now so I was not surprised to see some hands go up. "Bill, would you go first please?"

"I don't see why you have to go to all the trouble of messing with planning systems when you can accomplish the same thing by just increasing your manufacturing Lead

Time. That way, your raw materials arrive early giving you the safety stock you need."

"Ok" I answered, "let's look at your suggestion. Increasing manufacturing Lead Time (or Cycle Time) in your planning system tells purchasing to have raw materials in house earlier than actual need. It also tells your production planner to release work to the floor earlier than needed. Then what happens? Several things:"

- ❖ "The production planner looses faith in the planning system. In fact, the production planner replaces the planning system with his or her individual system working off-line with some tickler file to release production orders. Why not just disconnect the planning systems?"
- ❖ "Purchasing looses faith in the system. When the planning system defines a certain due date, the buyer knows that there is built in slack and is tempted to ignore, or at least, not treat action messages as critical."

"You have to ask yourself this question. Do I want my planning system to be credible, or is it just a guideline. If the latter is the case, the results will be increased costs, and the neutering of you planning system when you go to informal compensating techniques like overstated manufacturing Cycle Times. I've seen it happen repeatedly and so have you. It's your choice; I know that you feel more in control when you override the system. I know you feel you earn your pay when you are in control. I ask that you exercise that control, not by overriding the planning system, but by working on those things that need your skills, vendor pricing and quoted Lead Times."

Next came Tom. I nodded toward him and he started: "Look we all know that the real problem is the Cycle Time lengths that drive Lead Time lengths. When we balance lines and reduce Cycle Time then we will control the Lead Time. I agree that until then we compensate with inventory held at the cheapest point (preferable at the raw material vendors location and on their books). So all you've shown us is how to calculate the quantity of inventory needed, correct?"

"Close Tom", I replied, "but I am trying to get us to look at it differently. I want us to separate Lead Time and Cycle Time. I want us to attack Lead Time so that we reduce costs and free up resources to then go after Cycle Times using whatever methods you like. Why, because Lead Time lengths should be addressed separately. Why, because Lead Time lengths are the result of your, and your vendor's, business decisions and decisions are easier to change than processes. I once attended a seminar where the speaker bragged about reducing a Lead Time from 250 days to 125 days. To him it was inconceivable that both times were inappropriate. He had negotiated a 50% reduction, was he good or what? All of you are intelligent people; you're motivated to do the best job you can. You get a great deal of satisfaction and pride from being able to react quickly, and effectively to changes. What I'm pointing out removes that path to satisfaction and replaces it with another. To date, you have known that the planning system needed human interaction to correct its shortcomings. The good news has been that the system is highly reactive; the bad news is that the system is highly reactive. The methods I have shared (AMS and ILMS) filter planning systems so that the reactiveness occurs only when absolutely needed, which means that human intervention, occurs far less frequently. They do not simply show you how much inventory you need to provide One Day Lead Times; they systemize the calculation of the quantity and the use of the inventory needed to support One Day Lead Times. They eliminate Cycle Time from the equation. They systematize the fact that Lead Time and Cycle Times are separate issues, related but separate. More importantly, this is not about inventory, it is about changing the way we do business so that we can work more effectively to control our supply chains and serve our customers. Reduced inventory levels are just an additional benefit. Also Tom, remember what happened to the vendor who calculated Lead Time based on capacity and backlog? How the Lead Times grew? How the result changed each time, they calculated it? How they needed infinite flexibility to be able to respond to change in the market place?"

"Ok" I said, "look I'm not trying to be rough on anyone. I am trying to change the way you do business, and how you get personal satisfaction at the same time. You are all too good at what you do to be spending time chasing shadows. Look for real substance and pursue that."

"Let's assume you institute One Day Lead Times using the methods I described. The buyer's now have the time to use their skills to reduce the quantity of inventory needed to support their One Day Lead Times. That is, the buyer now has time to work with vendors getting them to One Day Lead Times while reducing their costs and reducing supply chain inventory. We know this process as negotiation."

"Negotiation is the art of insuring that each side sees the advantages of dealing with each other. For our purposes that means that vendors see the advantages of providing buyers with One Day quoted Lead Times. The process starts with vendor communication (or education if you prefer)."

"Effective communication is the key. Effective communication is the mutual understanding of words and terms. The buyer and vendor must agree on the following:" I pointed to the charts and read:

**"The definition of Lead Time.
Lead Time is the amount of time, defined by the vendor, to meet a request or demand."**

**"The purpose of Lead Time.
Lead Time defines the point in time when an action must be taken to insure the desired outcome."**

"The factors that drive Lead Time. Traditionally the vendor's view of its competitive position, its manufacturing strategy and the product's position in its life cycle drive Lead Time. The buyers job here is to insure that the vendors adopts the processes defined here."

"These points drive the context of all negotiations relative to Lead Time, as they have been the basis of our discussion to this point. All other perceived factors, capacity, economic lot sizing, and Cycle Time, etc. drive cost, quality, and inventory; they should not be allowed to drive quoted Lead Time length (review Section One). Vendors that will not accept these facts, will not be in a position provide One Day Lead Times. The buyer's communications skills insure that negotiations revolve around these points. The buyer communicates the costs associated with Lead Time to the vendor. To assist in this communication, buyers accumulate costs by vendor to help form the basis of future product specifications, and vendor selection. I am not suggesting an adversarial relationship. The vendor may be in such a strong competitive position that good relations must be maintained. I am stating that the vendor be made aware that the buyer understands the true factors driving the vendors quoted Lead Time. For each vendor the buyer uses the Lead Time matrix (Chapter 10) to define where the vendor has the advantage and to plan internal strategies to reduce the vendor's competitive advantage."

"Once the buyer identifies factors the vendor uses to drive Lead Time length, the buyer is in a position to determine if the Lead Time being quoted is supported by the vendors perception of those facts. Example: A vendor may build-to-stock but quote several weeks as the Lead Time. The facts do not support the quoted Lead Time so an area of opportunity is open. A path to taking advantage of the opportunity has been defined; now we need agreement."

- ✓ "Does the vendor understand that the quoted Lead Time means that the buyer must keep inventory to cover for expected changes?"
- ✓ "Does the vendor understand that inventory is lost, found, and otherwise fluctuates in quantity driving transactional activity levels?"
- ✓ "Does the Vendor understand that it is to his/hers advantage to maintain the lowest possible quoted Lead Time for their buyers?"

"In short does the vendor understand Section One? If not, educate. The goal; reach agreement on the factors that drive Lead Time. This base supports further advances. When the buyer finds that a vendor chooses to ignore facts because of some competitive advantage, the buyer must share the fact that he/she has become motivated to influence their own competitive disadvantage i.e., find another source."

"The buyer knows that the matrix is a snap shot in time. Business conditions constantly change so that yesterday's advantage becomes today's base line performance. A mature product changes to a declining product as demand changes. Buyers and vendors are continuously challenged to insure the factors that drive Lead Time reflect current business conditions. What I'm saying is use the matrix to focus negotiations. Get the vendors to specify the factors they believe drive their Lead Time then deal with the specifics one at a time."

"*Result*: some vendors will quote lower Lead Times, some will not, but the quoted Lead Times in the buyer's planning system must reflect the best the educated vendor will provide under today's business conditions. And the buyer must create:"

> ➤ "A list of those vendors that are open to further Lead Time improvement opportunities."
> ➤ "A list of those items/vendors that feel competitively strong enough to resist quoted Lead Time improvement opportunities."
> ➤ "A database of vendors, arranged by cost of doing business (Lead Time cost), for use by designers and others as part of the vendor selection process."

"In summary, look at the strong and weak points of negotiating as a stand alone technique and reconfigure it in your mind to see how it can be used as a part of the One Day Lead Time process."

Negotiations	
Strong Points	Weak Points
Low cost, does not add inventory.	Does not attack Cycle Time.
Forms a solid foundation for future improvements	Will not work with some vendors
May be the best result short of Cycle Time reduction.	Must be monitored so that changing conditions are reflected in the vendor's score.
	Takes a long time to implement across the entire vendor base.

"One final note before I talk about further improvements: The biggest roadblock I ran into, as I applied these techniques, grew from those, within my own organization, who claimed that a buyer should be able to negotiate quoted Lead Times lower without the use of compensating techniques. In short, you're a buyer, a tiger, go out there and beat your vendors into low Lead Times. That process exacerbates the weak points detailed above and since business conditions are always changing:"

- ✓ "Without a formal method of controlling inventory (calculated safety stock quantities), Murphy's law states that the safety stock carried by the vendor will be too little when needed, and too much when demand is soft."
- ✓ "The ego that forced the vendor to carry safety stock will be the same ego that will attempt to avoid responsibility for excess inventory."
- ✓ "The use of a buyer's competitive advantage to force a vendor to carry inventory is not Lead Time management, or inventory management and must, in the long term, cause the buyer and the vendor to suffer the consequences of non-managed programs."

- ✓ "Business conditions will change and the buyer will lose the competitive advantage. Vendors will remember being forced to carry inventory with no controlling process and the adversarial process will continue."
- ✓ "A Lead Time reduction program becomes a function of buyer's personality rather than a managed process."
- ✓ "Personality driven programs work to the advantage of the strong personality and the disadvantage of the company."

❖

❖

❖

Chapter 19

ELECTRONIC COMMERCE

"Earlier I talked about sharing scheduling and forecast information. As part of the AMS process, your customer's buyers agree to provide you with forecasts of their needs for your product(s). Let's look at how to share that information. But first, I'm going to review why."

- ❖ "Both AMS and ILMS use the same scheduling forecasts to calculate safety stock quantities, which are based on forecast error."
- ❖ "Forecast errors show if, and when, the provider of the information has built in any bias because normal forecast errors are random and roughly follow a bell curve."
- ❖ "Lack of bias builds credibility between buyer and vendor."

"As you have noticed, I have been working hard to let planning systems do what they do without human intervention. You have noticed that, in my view, human intervention increases as human interaction increases, i.e. when we leave the systems alone they do not require human intervention. You also noticed that modifying the planning system to use safety stock, as we want it to be used, blocks out messages to we humans. It sounds simplistic, I know, but to a large extent, one of the messages I am trying to impart is that the scheduling, expediting, and controlling work we have been doing adds no value to the supply chain.

Our expedites and changes, for the most part, only add costs. Effective management is management that does not smother. An effective manager does not control; an effective manager manages. Managing Electronic Commerce added to AMS reduces those costs."

"Electronic Commerce is a Cycle Time reduction tool. Like all good Cycle Time reduction tools, it eliminates the need for non-value adding operations. In this case, queue times while data from the buyer gets loaded into the vendors planning system, and visa-versa. Next, it automates those operations that cannot be eliminated. In this case, the actual interchange of data. What the buyer and vendor's systems do with the data exchanged does not concern the function of Electronic Commerce. Electronic Commerce's job is to improve the exchange of data. The goal of Electronic Commerce is the elimination of human element errors and the reduction in time consumed in communications. Electronic Commerce at its ideal performs:" I listed the items.

- **Purchase order placement/maintenance,**
- **Shipping order release,**
- **Shipment authorization,**
- **Receipts,**
- **Payment authorization, and**
- **Check issuance without human interface.**

"Companies use Electronic Commerce for all or some of these activities based on their equipment, abilities, and strategies. Some are listed on this slide."

EC Process	Description	Buyer Activities	Vendor Activities
File Transfer	Hard media (Disk) mailed between buyer and vendor.	Record demands and inventory on hard media.	Retrieve demand data from hard media and input into local system
		Receive and input, locally, shipping commitments from vendor.	Record shipping commitment on hard media.
PC Auto Fax	Data Faxed between buyer and vendor	Transmit demands and inventory via Fax.	Retrieve demand data from hard media and input into local system
		Receive Fax and input, locally, shipping commitments from vendor.	Record shipping commitment on hard media.
Systems Linkage (ANSI 830, 850, 862)	System to system communications	Part, or all, of procurement related transactions communicated directly between	Part, or all, of procurement related transactions communicated directly between systems.

"Many books have been published on the subject of Electronic Commerce so I will not get into setting up the process here. Electronic Commerce is an example of Cycle Time reduction. Absent AMS it may, or may not, affect the Lead Time quoted by a vendor in and of itself (remember, Lead Time length is a business decision). It does improve the flow of the information used to support Vendor Managed Inventory programs. It shows vendors how the buyer will exchange the information the vendor feels they need. Cycle Time improvements result in a reduction in the amount of inventory required to support a One Day quoted Lead Time. Since Electronic Commerce reduces the Cycle Time required in order placement and maintenance it by definition reduces inventory quantities (safety stock quantities). That is the reason that I keep restating that the ultimate method of Lead Time management is Cycle Time reduction; it is the Holy Grail."

"What is the minimum information that must be communicated?" asked Paul.

I answered, "Current inventory of the vendors product(s) and planned consumption per agreed to delivery intervals. Or, how many will the buyer use and when. Please note, I did not say how many the buyer wanted to be delivered each time but what the consumption rate was. The information comes from the buyers planning system and no hedge inventory can be allowed."

"Just a point of clarification if I may," said Bill. "Are you saying that the buyer has no input into the buying practices with the vendor?"

"No way," I responded. "The buyer negotiates price, stocking strategy, reviews and approves the vendors safety stock quantities, negotiates quality standards and measurements, and insures the overall reliability of the vendor. What the buyer does not do is become involved in the day-to-day workings of the relationship as regards to delivery quantities and delivery dates. The two planning systems monitor and control those activities using Electronic Commerce as the communication tool."

"OK," he continued. "Lets say that I am involved with a new product. Let's say further, that I have been instructed to have three months supply of all raw material on hand at start up to insure that we have enough and can cover for any problem. Are you saying that I am wrong to do as I have been instructed?"

"I believe in job security as much as the next person," I replied. "Do as you are instructed, however you have a responsibility to your management to share with them the costs associated with their decision. Let's face it; they are not accustomed to a world of One Day Lead Times. Historically they have had to hedge for the unforeseen. You now can present to them a cost effective alternative. This is what I recommend:" I checked off the list.

- ❖ **"Show the agreement between you and your vendor."**
- ❖ **"Show the actual results, in terms of inventory and transactional costs of you using AMS to support your customer's buyers."**
- ❖ **"Using two sets of numbers (your traditional method vs. One Day Lead Time methods), detail the savings potential."**

"If they still say no," I concluded, "then you do what you have to do, fair enough?"

"Ok" he said, "just one more clarification. Are you saying that the vendor can review and comment on the buyers inventory quantities?"

"Most definitely" I said. "In fact, a key ingredient of the Adaptive Master Scheduling portion of a One Day Lead Time process is to keep inventory quantities low. Failure to do so results in uncontrolled schedule changes and high transactional costs. The tighter the supply chain, in terms of inventory, the more effective that chain. That fact drives this process. When a vendor sees the buyer building hedge inventory he, or she, has the right and the duty to learn what is going on. My experience has been that most times it is caused by an 'off-system' need. The buyer has been told that an increase in schedule may occur and to be ready with inventory. The logic being that the inventory can always be worked off (reduced) later. Electronic Commerce forces everyone to use the planning system. That way, production scheduling, planning, purchasing and sales are all working from the same set of numbers. I have yet to see the 'off-system' as an effective way to run a business."

"Now Dave, you've completed the circle," commented Bill. "You're back to vendor managed inventories, the proven method for accomplishing yours goals without changing every ones planning systems, right?"

"Funny you should mention," I smiled. "That is just where I'm going next."

"But first lets look at a summary of Electronic commerce."

Electronic Commerce	
Strong Points	Weak Points
Reduces procurement costs.	Will not work with some vendors where limited systems resources exist.
Reduces procurement are receipt Cycle Times	
Improves the quality of data interchange.	Takes a long time to implement across the entire vendor base.
Reinforces Cycle Time reduction concepts for the buyer and the vendor.	
Builds on other Lead Time reduction techniques toward minimization of procurement Cycle Time.	

Chapter 20

VENDOR MANAGED INVENTORIES (VMI)

"First time listeners to this talk sometimes hear that I support Vendor Managed Inventories (VMI). That is, inventories held by vendors to accomplish two goals: 1) Support short Lead Times. 2) To keep inventory off the buyers books. I added this topic to show how traditional VMI ties into, and compares to, what I have already laid out. The first goal of the traditional Vendor Managed Inventory technique is to transfer ownership (financial and/or physical) from the buyer to the vendor. The theory is; the vendor would then be more motivated to control the amounts of inventory while the buyer minimizes financial exposure. That goal conflicts with the vendors attempt to move their finished product to the buyer to minimize their inventories and receive payment. There must be a business reason for the vendor to agree to hold inventory for the buyer. Too often, that reason has been the relative negotiating strength of the buyer. The result is VMI established inventory quantities, held by the vendor, were based on the dictates of the buyer. My experience showed buyers used nebulous terms to give maximum financial protection to themselves, i.e. "I don't care how much inventory you carry so long as I have a One Day Lead Time". Negotiations were, by definition, adversarial."

"And your point?" asked Bill, a wry smile on his face.

"My point is this," I replied. "Buyers who disassociate themselves from how a vendor accomplishes the tasks assigned losses cost saving potential. Most often, they add cost to the product they buy. Before I examine those facts let's look at some of the ways VMI is implemented.

This chart shows the general methods, in your world, you may vary slightly but most VMI practices fall into one of these categories."

VMI category	Attributes
Vendor stocking	The vendor maintains finished goods inventory, supplied to the buyer as defined contractually.
Vendor owned Inventory	The vendor maintains finished goods inventories at the buyer's site. Transfers product to the buyer as needed.
Staggered Orders	Vendor maintains finished goods and raw material as defined contractually.

- "*Vendor Stocking* – The buyer defines the frequency and quantities to be shipped from the vendor to the buyer. The buyer accepts physical and financial responsibility per the terms and conditions of the purchase order. The vendor monitors the buyer's inventory via Electronic Commerce and ships per the agreed to signal. The vendors base their quoted Lead Time on their order processing and transportation time and the dictates of the buyer. Inventories located at the vendors may, or may not, have a liability attached to them, based on the terms of the controlling contract, in either case the buyer's financial system does not track any financial responsibility. The vendor defines stocking levels to support quoted Lead Times. The caveat, the vendor agrees to meet any request from the buyer at the shortened One Day Lead Time."
- "*Vendor owned Inventory* – This technique mirrors Vendor Stocking except that the buyer has a quantity of finished goods inventory on site. Quantities kept at the vendor's site, and buyer's site may, or may not, be contractually defined, however the financial responsibility for that inventory does not

show on the buyer's books. The physical transfer of product from vendor to buyer occurs on a prearranged signal."

♦ I put up a new slide. *"Staggered Orders* – This technique, while delaying ownership of the finished product for the buyer, formally commits the buyer to increasingly greater portions of the vendors cost. A method of those commitments is the use of time zones."

Timeframe	Quantity commitment	Financial commitment
Forecast (Planning Zone)	None	None
Medium (Firm zone)	Quantity over difference of material Lead Time and manufacturing Cycle Time, i.e. if material Lead Time is 12 weeks and manufacturing Cycle time is 2 weeks the buyer commits to quantities from week 3 to week 12.	Full material cost for the given period of time with some allowance for quantity changes.
Short term (Frozen zone)	Quantity equal to the projected usage over the manufacturing Cycle Time	Full product price for the quantity.

"The buyer recommits (rolls) the governing purchase order each month and the vendor holds the inventory. The contract gives the buyer the right to change quantities at agreed upon percentage without liability (+/- 10% in frozen zone +/- 20% in firm zone). The following chart shows a history of three consecutive month's roll, (Given manufacturing Lead Time two weeks, Material Lead Time 10 weeks and weekly deliveries):"

Staggered Order VMI

Key: ▨ Frozen ▨   Firm   Forecast

January-97		February-97		March-97	
Time Zone/dates	Qty	Time Zone/dates	Qty	Time Zone/dates	Qty
1/6	50	2/3	62	3/3	61
1/13	50	2/10	55	3/10	55
1/20	50	2/17	47	3/17	53
1/27	50	2/24	58	3/24	50
2/3	60	3/3	61	3/31	55
2/10	55	3/10	55	4/7	55
2/17	45	3/17	53	4/14	60
2/24	60	3/24	50	4/21	60
3/3	60	3/31	55	4/28	50
3/10	50	4/7	55	5/5	55
3/17	65	4/14	60	5/12	60
3/24	50	4/21	60	5/19	63
3/31	55	4/28	50	5/26	65
4/7	200	5/5	210	6/2	210
4/14		5/12		6/9	
4/21		5/19		6/16	
4/28		5/26		6/23	
5/5	210	6/2	210	6/30	220

"Note: The forecast zone uses larger demand buckets because those forecasts are further in the future (less accurate) and are used for planning (capacity) purposes only."

The vendor enforces quantity commitments and materials liabilities on the buyer upon order cancellation and/or, when the buyer's projected timing and quantities are not met."

"Commitments for materials can be set to include only long Lead Time components so the entire bill of materials need not be covered. The quantities that the buyer commits to are in line with short-term quantity needs. This allows buyer and vendor to work closely together in determining what and how much each needs to insure that risks are managed. This also means that the initial contract negotiations can take a long time. I have used a planning system that automates the process of updating the orders, but not all purchasing planning systems have this option built-in. If the planning system does not automatically notify the buyer of the need to update an open order the buyer must implement a manual tickler method as a reminder to update staggered orders. In short:"

Staggered Orders	
Strong Points	Weak Points
Reduces buyer commitments	Does not attack Cycle Time.
Gives vendors strong commitments and long range visibility	Unless automated, updates are time consuming.
Quantifies risk management	Detailing risk and enforcement of zones takes a long time to negotiate and implement across the entire vendor base.

New VMI "Now lets get to my points regarding costs. True AMS is like a Vendor Managed Inventory program. The difference between traditional VMI and new VMI using Adaptive Master Scheduling lies in the fact that the new VMI provides the business case justification for the vendor. The vendor quantifies the advantages in terms of the reduction in total inventory quantities and the reduction in the transactional costs using the methods I showed in Section 1, namely lower transactional costs, and less production disruption caused by trying to react to changing priorities. AMS builds on these cost savings with its production schedule averaging component. Empirically defining inventory quantities, using statistical forecast error calculations, provides the management tool (justification) not present in traditional VMI. AMS algorithms, added to the planning system of each vendor in the supply chain, statistically derive and systemically control inventory quantities. Traditional VMI provides no systemic control of inventory. A vendor need only calculate forecast error driven buffer stock and compare that to however he/she calculates VMI inventory to quantify the difference. If the entire supply chain does not use One Day Lead Time methods, then adding the Item Level Master Scheduling program provides additional savings. Said simply, One Day Lead Times is a VMI program that drives quantifiable savings for the vendor and the buyer."

"Again to more directly address Bill's point, why do I care how the vendor meets my needs as long as they are met? I care because as a buyer I pay for vendor's costs one way or another. If the buyer does not pay as part of the unit price, then the vendor must absorb the costs. Absorbing cost is not the way to stay in business. If you value long-term relations with vendors, you must be concerned with their ability to make a reasonable profit. We have just defined the point where the buyer can, and should, be exerting effort. Not negotiating Lead Times, but working with vendors on cost, price, and quality."

"One last point for the vendors relative to VMI. Varying rates of product consumption by buyers of the same product can send false consumption messages to the vendor. False consumption messages leads to high inventories when the vendor does not hold the inventory and provide One Day Lead Times. Said another way, inventory held by the vendor who quotes a short Lead Times is less than the inventory produced by the vendor who ships inventory to the buyer and quotes longer Lead Times. This means that buyer who buys on consignment returns less unsold inventory. The buyer who buys for sale, marks down less unsold inventory in the event of less than anticipated sales rates. Moreover, the vendor, who provides the product, has a closer link to actual consumption rates of his/her product controlling the manufacturing rate."

"A side-by-side comparison shows how this happens (I made the chart the last page of this chapter so that you can examine it as I develop the advantages). Lets look at Vendor A whose quoted Lead Time is three months (12 weeks) against a Vendor B whose quoted Lead Time is one week. Both supply the same buyers, the rate of consumption forecast for each is 100/week, and the stocking strategy is the same for Vendor A's product and Vendor B's product, 8 weeks. Each vendor manufactures in lot sizes of 5000. The buyers of Vendor B communicate forecasted and actual consumption via Electronic Commerce."

"The differences begin at the first order. Due to Vendor A's 12 week quoted Lead Time, buyers could not purchase to their stocking strategy, they had to buy enough to cover the vendors Lead Time and place another order for 12 week out at 800 units (Stocking strategy times forecasted consumption). Vendor B has orders that fill the buyers buy policy, based on the forecast of 100/week."

"In week 11 Vendor B supports higher than forecasted demand from inventory and the buyer is happy. Buyer East, in Vendor A's supply chain, has run out of product and must stop production or turn away consumers."

"Week 13 Vendor A ships the orders that were made at Lead Time (12 weeks ago). Buyer East has been out of stock and is not happy. Buyers Middle and West are flooded with excess inventory. Lastly, vendor A has created its own excess inventory."

"By the time this example calendar ran out there were 5135 extra units in supply chain inventory and no happy buyers for supply chain A. Meanwhile, back at chain B, the buyers are able to order based on historical consumption and their stocking strategy of 8 weeks. Inventory levels are managed; it's a Win-Win situation."

"But you say, that can be accomplished using any VMI strategy," a stated rhetorically. "My answer is 'no way.' You only think they are the same. AMS controls the quantity of inventory held by the suppler. AMS never allows that quantity to grow out of control, or get to zero."

"Well that's it folks, let me wrap up."

Managing Inventory • 217

Vendor A (12 week Lead Time)

Week #	Made	Buyer East			Buyer Middle			Buyer West			Chain A
		Bought	Sold	Inv.	Bought	Sold	Inv.	Bought	Sold	Inv.	Inv.
1	5000	1200	100	1100	1200	80	1120	1200	90	1110	4730
2			120	980		70	1050		80	1030	4460
3			110	870		90	960		85	945	4175
4			140	730		100	860		102	843	3833
5			110	620		60	800		75	768	3588
6			125	495		75	725		80	688	3308
7			150	345		90	635		62	626	3006
8			135	210		80	545		66	560	2725
9			110	100		95	450		65	495	2455
11			100	0		80	370		70	425	2205
12				0		80	290		65	360	2060
13	5000	1200	160	1140	1200	75	1415	1200	68	1492	6757
14			105	1035		80	1335		70	1422	6502
15			100	935		70	1265		72	1350	6260
16			110	825		65	1200		65	1285	6020
17			100	725		70	1130		70	1215	5780

Vendor B (1 week Lead Time)

Week #	Made	Buyer East			Buyer Middle			Buyer West			Chain B
		Bought	Sold	Inv.	Bought	Sold	Inv.	Bought	Sold	Inv.	Inv.
1	5000	800	100	700	800	80	720	800	90	710	4730
2			120	980		70	1050		80	1030	4460
3			110	870		90	960		85	945	4175
4			140	730		100	860		102	843	3833
5			110	620		60	800		75	768	3588
6			125	495		75	725		80	688	3308
7			150	345		90	635		62	626	3006
8			135	210		80	545		66	560	2725
9			110	100		95	450		65	495	2455
11		980	120	960		80	370		70	425	2185
12			120	840		80	290		65	360	1920
13			115	725		75	215		68	300	1662
14			110	615		80	135		70	235	1402
15			115	500		70	75		72	165	1145
16			110	390		65	10		65	100	905
17			100	290	635	70	575		70	30	665

Chapter 21

WRAP-UP

"My goal, from the beginning, has been to have Lead Time length removed from negotiations. Lead Time length should be one day, no longer. It costs buyers and vendors too much to have it otherwise. I have shown why it is possible. I have shown how to do it."

"Cycle Time drives the amount of inventory required to support One Day Lead Times. One uses Cycle Time reduction techniques to continually reduce the quantity of inventory. So, the cost of Cycle Time is the amount of finished goods inventory. The cost of vendors Lead Time is the amount of purchased materials safety stock carried. I arrived at these facts by showing:"

1) "Lead Time exists to direct when an action should take place to insure a desired result."
2) "Lead Times, entered into a planning system must be credible, accurate and timely or they cannot perform their defined task."
3) "Up to now, these facts did not control our decisions because our life experiences contradicted them. In life, Lead Time gives a safety cushion; it insures we do not disappoint the one counting on us. In business, the safety cushion, adds costs, adds inventory, and neuters planning systems."
4) "Cycle Time is the amount of time elapsed to complete an operation or is the sum of times assigned or allocated to complete a process."

5) "Cycle Time is to Lead Time as cost is to price. They are related but, just as cost does not drive selling price, Cycle Time does not drive Lead Time. Lead Time can be longer than, shorter than, or equal to product Cycle Time."
6) "As Lead Time length increases vendors and buyer's costs (transactional activities and inventories) increase, production planning becomes reactive, and customer service suffers, because the buyer is forced to forecast further into the future. The longer the forecast period the greater the probability of change."
7) "An examination of cause and effect shows that traditional Lead Time length rationale cannot be justified. Cycle Time cannot drive Lead Time because demand does not consistently match capacity. Because demand rates vary, Cycle Times vary because one element of product Cycle Time is queue (waiting for available capacity). Variable Lead Times neuter planning systems."
8) "Capacity cannot drive Lead Time length because:"
   a) "Capacity loads of less than 100% equal the lowest Lead Times because the lowest the Lead Time can be is the Cycle Time required to produce a product. So there can be no direct correlation between capacity and Lead Time length as capacity drops below 100%. Low demand also means excess capacity."
   b) "High demand drives increasing Cycle Time that drives the Lead Time spiral that creates false demand as buyer's hedge to protect their supply of product."

9) "Buyers attempt to influence Lead Time length when they communicate the parameters of a quote to vendors. Because the process is neither defined nor consistent, inconsistent Lead Times result."
10) "Vendors set Lead Time Length based on their perception of the market. Their competitive advantage, manufacturing strategy, and the position of the product in its life cycle define what Lead Time the vendor will quote."

"Cycle Time length is the result of a mathematical calculation (the addition of Cycle Time and/or Lead Time elements),

Lead Time length is the result of a business decision."

11) "A vendor who has inventory can quote a shorter Lead Time than one without inventory. One source of inventory is safety stock. The trick is determining how much inventory (safety stock) and where it is located. The second source of inventory is the stock strategy of the buyer. Since production buyers buy in quantities greater than their immediate needs, they have available inventory one-half of the time."
12) "Safety stock is the quantity of an item set aside to cover for changes in supply or demand inside quoted Lead Time. The problem is that planning systems consume safety stock as a method of protecting that inventory from use. Therefore, planning system messages drive the buyer (and sometimes the vendor) into actions as if there was no safety stock."
13) "Setting Lead Time lengths at one day satisfy the definitions and criteria of Lead Time. I have done it and the results can be replicated by anyone."

14) "The One Day Lead Times Process:"
   a) "First step work with your current system to make sure that the Lead Time you quote is accurate, adhered to and timely. This step reduces your quoted Lead Time by recognizing inventories created by stocking strategies."
   b) "Use statistical forecast error calculation to define the amount of safety stock required to meet a specified service level."
   c) "Use a quantity of finished goods safety stock to allow you to quote one day Lead Times. Modify your planning system (Adaptive Master Scheduling) to allow the use of the safety stock. Work with your customers to remove inventory from the supply chain."
   d) "Further reduce inventories by having safety stock of all purchased items. Item Level Master Scheduling insures that your planning system allows for the systemic use of raw material safety stock. As raw material safety stock increases, finished goods safety stock decreases. Since finished goods cost more than raw materials the total amount of inventory decreases."
   e) "Start working with your vendors to help them reach One Day quoted Lead Times. Know what they base their Lead Time on, and then educate them on the effects of Lead Time length."
   f) "Use Cycle Time reductions to further reduce inventory levels."
   g) "Transfer all the above to you vendors as Vendor Managed Inventory. Insure that the process that backs up VMI is statistically sound and systemic."

"Lead Time management then, becomes the key to Cycle Time reduction. Managing Lead Times of one day means that Cycle Times are kept as low as possible so that inventory quantities are as low as possible."

"The steps in the One Day Lead Time Process are:"

1. "Practical Lead Time: Quoted Lead Times must be modified to show the effects of current inventories (buying policies and Safety Stocks). Practical Lead Times result in lower quoted Lead Times with no change in business practices."
2. "Adaptive Master Scheduling: Finished goods inventory (based on the product Cycle Time), at the vendor's, drives low quoted Lead Times to the next supply chain link. That link then lowers the inventory quantity of raw materials (the vendors finished goods) to a level not to exceed the vendors quoted Lead Time in days of supply."
3. "Item Level master Scheduling: Safety stocks of purchased goods compensate for vendor Lead Time lengths and vendor performance. Lower finished goods safety stock quantities based on the reduction in product Cycle Time. The purchase goods Lead Time length component is zero therefore, the product Cycle Time is equal to manufacturing Cycle Time."
4. "Implement Electronic Commence to improve communications and eliminate human errors."
5. "Implement continuous improvement through Cycle Time reduction techniques."

"I'll close as I started." I put up my opening slide:

Imagine what your professional life would be like if all Lead Time lengths were One Day

"The charts that follow look at techniques and results first, then a comparison of the techniques shown. Thank you for your attention, and good luck to you as you take control of Lead Time length."

Managing Inventory • 225

Vendor A (12 week Lead Time)

Week #	Made	Buyer East			Buyer Middle			Buyer West			Chain A
		Bought	Sold	Inv.	Bought	Sold	Inv.	Bought	Sold	Inv.	Inv.
1	5000	1200	100	1100	1200	80	1120	1200	90	1110	4730
2			120	980		70	1050		80	1030	4460
3			110	870		90	960		85	945	4175
4			140	730		100	860		102	843	3833
5			110	620		60	800		75	768	3588
6			125	495		75	725		80	688	3308
7			150	345		90	635		62	626	3006
8			135	210		80	545		66	560	2725
9			110	100		95	450		65	495	2455
11			100	0		80	370		70	425	2205
12				0		80	290		65	360	2060
13	5000	1200	160	1140	1200	75	1415	1200	68	1492	6757
14			105	1035		80	1335		70	1422	6502
15			100	935		70	1265		72	1350	6260
16			110	825		65	1200		65	1285	6020
17			100	725		70	1130		70	1215	5780

Vendor B (1 week Lead Time)

Week #	Made	Buyer East			Buyer Middle			Buyer West			Chain B
		Bought	Sold	Inv.	Bought	Sold	Inv.	Bought	Sold	Inv.	Inv.
1	5000	800	100	700	800	80	720	800	90	710	4730
2			120	980		70	1050		80	1030	4460
3			110	870		90	960		85	945	4175
4			140	730		100	860		102	843	3833
5			110	620		60	800		75	768	3588
6			125	495		75	725		80	688	3308
7			150	345		90	635		62	626	3006
8			135	210		80	545		66	560	2725
9			110	100		95	450		65	495	2455
11		980	120	960		80	370		70	425	2185
12			120	840		80	290		65	360	1920
13			115	725		75	215		68	300	1662
14			110	615		80	135		70	235	1402
15			115	500		70	75		72	165	1145
16			110	390		65	10		65	100	905
17			100	290	635	70	575		70	30	665

Managing Inventory • 227

Technique	Effect on Inventory	Effect on Transactions	Effect on Responsiveness	Costs to vendor	Ease of Implementation
Practical Lead Times	No effect on inventory for vendor, some lowering of inventory for buyer.	None	Improved to reflect current stocking strategies.	None	Software modification.
Lead Time verification			None Forms baseline		
Adaptive Master Scheduling	Customer inventories greatly reduced. Vendor inventories may increase.	Less transactional activity between vendor and customer.	Greatly enhanced	Vendor absorbs cost of finished goods inventory, balanced against more stable demand profile, lower transactions, improved customer relations	Software purchased or developed. Contract negotiation with each customer.
Item Level Master Scheduling	Raw materials inventories reduced, Finished goods inventories greatly reduced.	Less transactional activity between vendor and customer.	If no AMS greatly improved. If added to AMS no change.	Software implementation	Software purchased or developed. Contract negotiation with each customer.
Electronic Commerce	None	Greatly reduced, more accurate.	None	System improvements.	Difficult: as vendor capabilities vary, different EC tools are used.
Cycle Time reduction	Greatly improved	Reduced.	Based on business practices of each vendor.	Cost reduced, quality improved, inventories reduced.	Difficult to work through an entire vendor base.

❖

❖

❖

Chapter 22

MANAGING INVENTORY WITH AN INTEGRATED SUPPLY CHAIN

Each link in a supply chain is both vendor (shaded area) and buyer (clear area).

The vendor portion includes all the activities of the sales/marketing and manufacturing functions in a link.

The buyer portion includes all activities of the Buyer function.

A typical supply chain link

| Sales/Marketing |
| Manufacturing |
| Buyer |

Simple Supply Chain

Key: Lines with arrows represent lines of communication and product flow. Dashes in the line represent communication problems along the line caused by quoted Lead Time length. The greater the quoted Lead Time the larger the gaps in the communication line. A solid line means that any communication is accepted and acted on as requested.

The supply chain path follows the circled number 1 to 7.

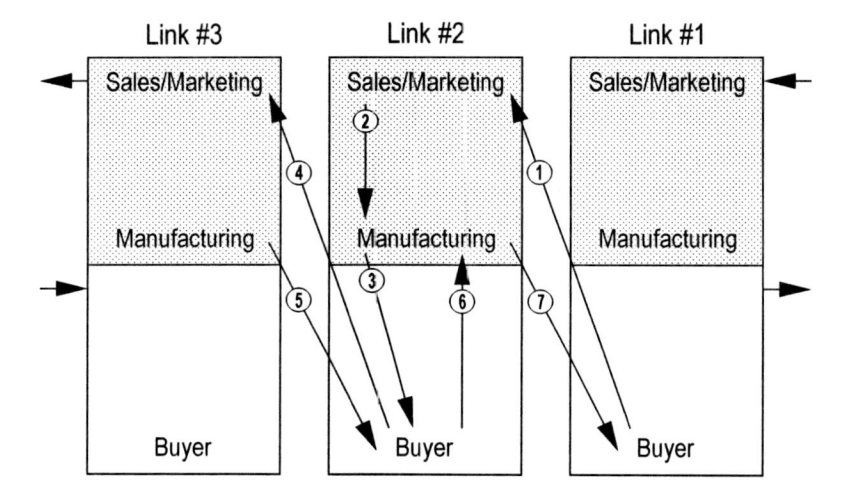

Link #3	Link #2	Link #1
Sales/Marketing	Sales/Marketing ②	Sales/Marketing
Manufacturing ④	Manufacturing ③	Manufacturing ①
⑤	⑥ ⑦	
Buyer	Buyer	Buyer

Generally, the activities, and communications, in a simple supply chain follow this path:

1. The buyer in Link #1 orders products from vendor Link #2 sales.
2. The Link #2 sale's receives orders and passes them, through the planning system, to manufacturing.
3. The planning system of manufacturing passes requests for necessary raw material to buyer.
4. The buyer in Link #2 sends orders to Link #3 sales for raw materials.
5. The Link #3 fills the orders and ship to the Link #2 buyer.
6. The Link #2 buyer forewords the raw material to manufacturing who processes them into finished product
7. Link #2 then ships the finished product to the Link #1 buyer.

Typical Supply Chain

(Not Integrated)

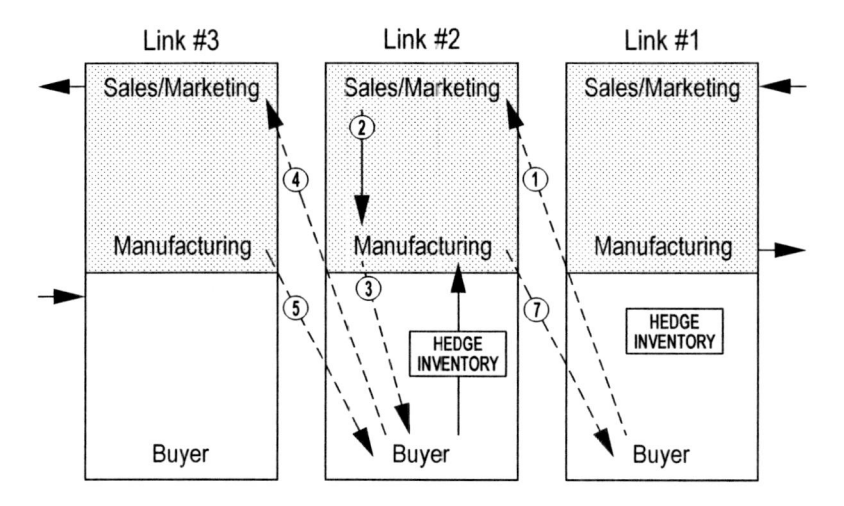

	Link #3	Link #2	Link #1
	Sales/Marketing	Sales/Marketing	Sales/Marketing
	Manufacturing	Manufacturing	Manufacturing
		HEDGE INVENTORY	HEDGE INVENTORY
	Buyer	Buyer	Buyer

When Vendor Lead Time lengths conflict with needs, as perceived by buyers, communications gaps appear. The vendor unable, or unwilling, to react as requested by the buyer forces the buyer to protect against change by holding inventory. The buyer bases the inventory (hedge) quantity on experience. For this reason hedge inventory quantities are uncontrolled. Uncontrolled inventory quantities, by definition, do not always allow the vendor to meet buyer's needs. They only add costs. Because the quantities are uncontrolled, additional costs accumulate as buyer and sellers try to negotiate quantities and schedules to meet ever-changing needs. The supply chain looks like the above.

1. The buyer in Link #1 orders products from vendor Link #2 sales.
2. The Link #2 sale's receives orders and passes them, through the planning system, to manufacturing.
3. In Link #2, the planning system of manufacturing passes requests for necessary raw material to buyer.
4. The buyer in Link #2 sends orders to Link #3 sales for raw materials.
5. The Link #3 fills the orders and ships to the Link #2 buyer.
6. The Link #2 buyer forewords the raw material to manufacturing who processes them into finished product. When the quantity of raw material does not meet the manufacturing needs the buyer relies on hedge inventory fill the gap.
7. Link #2 then ships the finished product to the Link #1 buyer. When the quantity shipped does not meet the Link #1 buyer's needs, that buyer relies on hedge inventory fill the gap.

Uncontrolled inventories (hedge inventories), do not meet all needs. The only way to be sure there will always be sufficient inventory to meet needs is to have an infinite quantity of all materials or to never allow a buyer to change a request inside quoted Lead Time. Buyers will always need flexibility to change, and infinite inventory is not practical, therefore another process must be implemented.

Adaptive Master Scheduling

(Partial Integration)

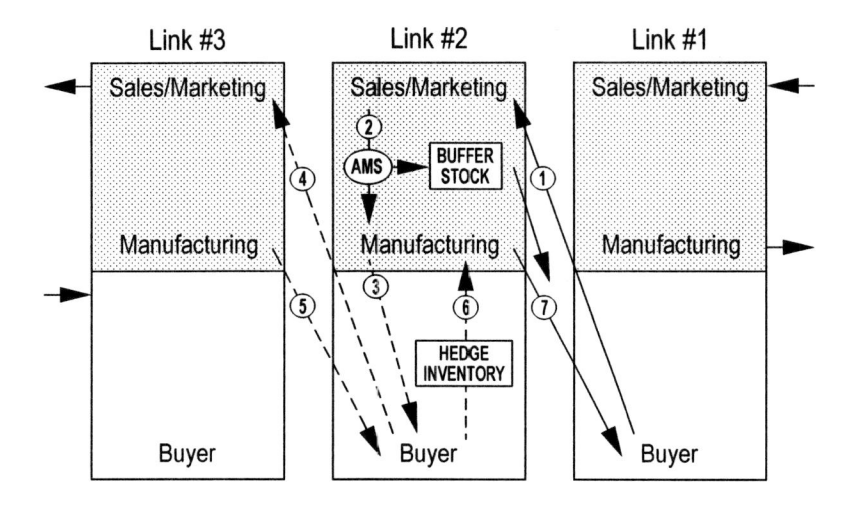

[Diagram showing three Links (#3, #2, #1), each with Sales/Marketing, Manufacturing, and Buyer sections. Link #2 contains AMS, BUFFER STOCK, and HEDGE INVENTORY elements, with numbered flows 1-7 between the links.]

AMS allows Link #2 to quote One Day Lead Times to Link #1.

1. The Link #1 places orders (quantities and requested delivery dates), with Link #2 based on One Day Lead Times. Link #1 provides forecasts of their needs for products based on the Cycle Times provided by Link #2. Link #1 no longer needs hedge inventory.
2. The Link #2 receives orders and passes them, through the planning system, to manufacturing. AMS modifies the planning system smoothing out the demands sent to manufacturing. AMS also controls a quantity of buffer stock (controlled inventory) of finished product.

3. Link #2 manufacturing passes smoothed requests for necessary raw material to the buyer.
4. Link #2 Buyer sends orders to Link #3 based on the quoted Lead Time of Link #3. The Link #2 buyers gets the benefit of less volatility in the raw material demand profile because of the demand smoothing performed by AMS prior to manufacturing.
5. The Link #3 fills the orders from buyer and ships to Link #2.
6. The Link #2 buyer forewords the raw material to manufacturing who processes them into finished product. When the quantity of raw material does not meet the manufacturing needs the buyer relies on hedge inventory fill the gap.
7. Link #2 then ships the finished product to the Link #1 buyer. If Link #1 buyer needs a quantity greater than produced by manufacturing the buffer stock controlled by AMS provides the finished product to meet that need. To Link #1 buyer, the Link #2 product Lead Time is One Day.

AMS is a buffer between Link #1 and all Lead Times and Cycle Times that affected Link #2's ability to react to change eliminating the costs of negotiating change. AMS reduced the total quantity of finished goods inventory and eliminated the need for the Hedge Inventory of finished goods at the Link #1's location.

Item Level Master Scheduling
(Full Integration)

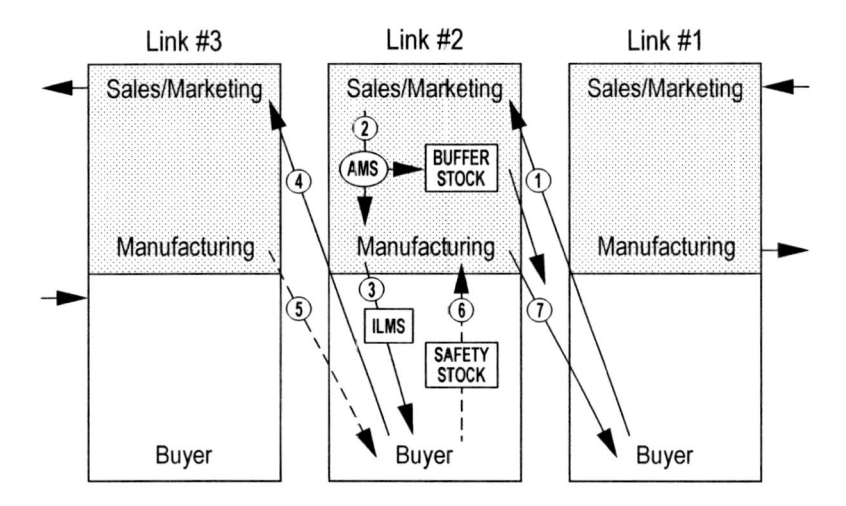

[Diagram showing three Links (#3, #2, #1) each containing Sales/Marketing, Manufacturing, and Buyer sections. Link #2 contains AMS, BUFFER STOCK, ILMS, and SAFETY STOCK components with numbered arrows (1-7) showing flows between the Links.]

ILMS compensates for the Lead Time between the Link #2 and Link #3 by the correct use of safety stock (controlled inventory). ILMS acts as a filter between the Link #2's manufacturing and Buyer organizations replacing much of the finished goods inventory with raw material safety stock.

1. The Link #1 places orders (quantities and requested delivery dates), with Link #2 based on One Day Lead Times. Link #1 provides forecasts of their needs for products based on the Cycle Times provided by Link #2.

2. The Link #2 receives orders and passes them, through the planning system, to manufacturing. AMS modifies the planning system smoothing out the demands sent to manufacturing. AMS also controls a quantity of buffer stock (controlled inventory) of finished product.
3. Manufacturing passes smoothed requests for necessary raw material to Buyer.
4. ILMS establishes controlled safety stock quantities of raw materials from Link #3. ILMS filters raw material requests from manufacturing so that the buyer need not communicate any need, or change, inside Link #3's quoted Lead Time. Link #2 buyer sends new orders to Link #3 based on the quoted Lead Time of Link #3. The Link #2 buyers gets the benefit of less volatility in the raw material demand profile because of the demand smoothing performed by AMS prior to manufacturing.
5. The Link #3 fills the orders from Buyer and ships to the Link #2.
6. The Link #2 buyer forewords the raw material to manufacturing who processes them into finished product. When the quantity of raw material does not meet the manufacturing needs, raw material safety stock controlled by ILMS fills that need.
7. Link #2 then ships the finished product to the Link #1 buyer. If Link #1 buyer needs a quantity greater than produced by manufacturing the buffer stock controlled by AMS provide the finished product to meet that need. To Link #1 buyer, the Link #2 product Lead Time is One Day.

Managed Supply Chain

(Fully Integrated)

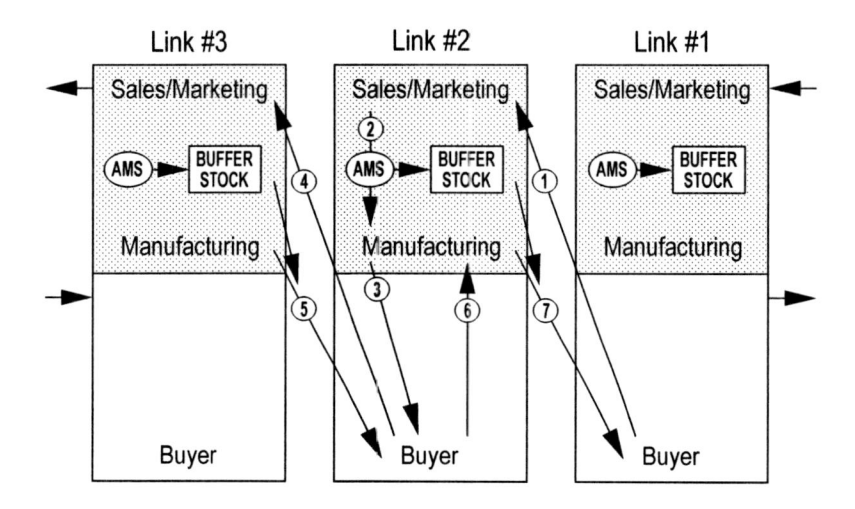

[Diagram: Three links (Link #3, Link #2, Link #1) each containing Sales/Marketing, AMS → BUFFER STOCK, Manufacturing, and Buyer, connected by numbered arrows ①–⑦.]

The ideal supply contains links that all use AMS to support One Day Lead Times and fully integrate each link in the supply chain systemically. The results are:

- $ All links managed inventory through empirically defined and systemically control inventory quantities.
- $ All links reap reduced procurement and planning costs
- $ All links take advantage of improved communications.
- $ All links have resources freed up to pursue Cycle Time reduction.

Managing Inventory • 239

1. The Link #1 places orders (quantities and requested delivery dates), with Link #2 based on One Day Lead Times. Link #1 provides forecasts of their needs for products based on the Cycle Times provided by Link #2.
2. The Link #2 receives orders and passes them, through the planning system, to manufacturing. AMS modifies the planning system smoothing out the demands sent to manufacturing. AMS also controls a quantity of buffer stock (controlled inventory) of finished product.
3. Manufacturing passes smoothed requests for necessary raw material to Buyer.
4. Link #2 buyer sends orders to Link #3 based on One Day quoted Lead Time of Link #3. The Link #2 buyers gets the benefit of less volatility in the raw material demand profile because of the demand smoothing performed by AMS prior to manufacturing.
5. The Link #3 fills the orders from Buyer and ships to the Link #2 with manufactured product supplemented, as needed, by buffer stock controlled by AMS.
6. The Link #2 buyer forewords the raw material to manufacturing who processes them into finished product.
7. Link #2 then ships the finished product to the Link #1 buyer. If Link #1 buyer needs a quantity greater than produced by manufacturing the buffer stock controlled by AMS provide the finished product to meet that need. To Link #1 buyer, the Link #2 product Lead Time is One Day.

The ideal eliminates communications problems and greatly reduces the quantity of inventory required to support highly flexible and reactive manufacturing.   ❖

Printed in the United States
5526